The Asquinn Twins
Book Three

No Greener Pastures

Grace Brooks

Earthly Stories with a Heavenly Meaning

The Asquinn Twins Book 3: No Greener Pastures

Original Copyright©2014: Heather Radford AKA Grace Brooks
All right to the contents of this book are reserved for the author

Published By Parables
June, 2018

All Rights Reserved. No part of this book may be reproduced or utilized in any form or by any means, electronic or mechanical, including photocopying, recording, or by any information storage and retrieval system, without permission in writing from the author.

Unless otherwise specified Scripture quotations are taken from the authorized version of the King James Bible.

First Edition   2014 / Heather Radford AKA Grace Brooks
This Edition   2018 / Grace Brooks

ISBN 978-1-945698-59-0

Printed in the United States of America

Readers should be aware that Internet Web sites offered as citations and/or sources for further information may have been changed or disappeared between the time this was written and when it is read.

The Asquinn Twins
Book Three

No Greener Pastures

Grace Brooks

PUBLISHED by PARABLES
Earthly Stories with a Heavenly Meaning

GRACE BROOKS

Dedication

The Asquinn Twins: No Greener Pastures is a work of fiction, which means all the characters are conjured out of my imagination and there are no real life counterparts. Anyone who knows the James Bay Frontier or Temiskaming District areas in the northern portion of the province of Ontario, Canada, will recognize the setting for this story and the series. Although I have used the right names for most of the towns, cities and rivers, I used a fictitious name for the town in my story.

But the idea for the series did spring from an incident concerning the Ontario Provincial Police, Mom, and me that nipped my life of crime in the bud. For this, I will be forever grateful and hold deep respect for them. I will not say which one of the occurrences in the series almost duplicates my brush with the law.

Ontario should be grateful they have the Ontario Provincial Police, and it's to this police force I dedicate the entire series.

One

Alone in Forest Lake

The three of them stood up.

"Thank you, Martin Asquinn, Mrs. Asquinn, for your interest in adopting."

"Thank you for taking the time to visit us, Mrs. Moore," Audrey said.

Mrs. Moore gathered up all the papers in front of her and returned them to her black briefcase. She started towards the door.

Outside the door, Mrs. Moore paused. Martin's gaze followed hers as she looked up at the upper level. "What's up there?"

"I will do better than tell you, I'll show you," Martin said and waved his hand for her up follow. "Come with me."

Audrey trailed her husband and Mrs. Moore up the staircase which levelled out into a hallway and one door. Martin knocked.

"Come in, Martin, Audrey," a female voice called.

Martin opened the door and allowed the child care worker, then Audrey, to enter first.

"Mrs. Moore, this is my younger brother, Eric, and his wife June, and baby Gay-Anne.

June, Eric, this is Mrs. Moore, the adoption lady. I was just showing her the place." Audrey remained behind as Martin showed the woman around.

"This apartment is almost as big as ours downstairs, only this one has two bedrooms."

Martin waited until they were back in Eric and June's hearing range to say the rest. "Our plans are to integrate this upper apartment into the rest of the house and have one big house to accommodate an expanding family."

"Are you officially notifying us we will have to move out?" Eric asked.

"Sorry, brother, but yes," Martin said.

"And you own the building?" Mrs. Moore said.

"Yes," Martin answered.

Mrs. Moore smiled, taking in all four. "Thank you for your time," she said, then left and headed back downstairs.

"We will keep your names on the list concerning adopting," Mrs. Moore said when they were outside.

"Thank you, again. Good afternoon, Mrs. Moore," Audrey said. "Good afternoon," Mrs. Moore replied.

As soon as Mrs. Moore's car had disappeared down the street, Audrey turned to Martin and rested her head on his chest with tears in her eyes.

"Adopting, darling," she said. "We are waiting to adopt a child."

Later that afternoon, Martin and Audrey prepared to visit. Audrey pulled the hood of her knee-length, down-filled parka up and waited as Martin zipped up his coat, pulled on his mittens, then opened the inside door. "You first."

Audrey smiled. "Thanks, Martin."

Martin opened the solid storm door leading outside and followed Audrey out. The heavy storm door closed behind Martin. In late January, the lawn was under a deep cover of snow.

Audrey reached out for Martin's hand as she stepped onto the icy gravel driveway. He steadied her and kept her from falling on the ice as they followed it to Forest Lake's main road.

The couple walked the short distance to the bottom of Golden Ridge where the church stood. They'd made their way up the hill to the manse and around to the back entrance when Martin heard the sound of harness bells jingling. He and Audrey looked in that direction.

A pair of brown horses, with shaggy winter coats, trotted easily through the snow pulling what appeared to be a giant rolling pin. In fact, it was a snow roller, made from wooden slates and steel spokes.

As the outfit came into view where the trees alongside the road thinned and Martin and Audrey got a better view, Martin waved at the driver. Mr. Greene waved back from his seat on top of the roller.

Martin and Audrey smiled at each other as Mr. Greene passed by, the jingling bells fastened to the shafts the harnesses were snapped on to, and from the harnesses themselves, increasing in volume on the way by then fading away.

Arriving at the portion of the road by the crossing below Golden Ridge, Mr. Greene turned the horses into the snow chocked railroad approach and turned the team around on the rail road tracks. Once they were turned, he shouted at the animals and started them once more, down the snow packed road, towards home.

"I've watched Chester Greene pack the snow on that unplowed section of road for many winters now, but I don't grow tired of watching the horses work."

"The bells are exciting, too," Audrey said.

Martin heard shouting coming from the direction of the church. He and Audrey looked in that direction. More shouting.

"You go on inside," Martin said to Audrey.

Martin jogged to the church. He climbed the steps, opened the front door and walked towards the sanctuary door. He heard more shouting. He peeked into the sanctuary and got the surprise of his life when his gaze fell on a little boy about three years old, and his mother standing in the middle pew row. She held a year-old baby in her arms. But neither were kneeling or praying.

"What are you doing here, Murray Asquinn?" the mother scolded. "I forbade you to come to this church. You, I, and Kirk go somewhere else."

Martin walked down the aisle and gently touched the lady's shoulder.

"It's nice to see you, Sherry," Martin whispered. "The door is always open. Whether you attend here or not, anyone can come in at any time." Martin hugged the three-year-old.

"I'm praying for Mommy and Daddy. Will you pray with me, Uncle Martin? Please?"

Sherry tossed her fair hair and her hazel eyes snapped with anger. "Do you think God even hears our prayers?"

"Oh, I'm certain he does."

"I mean, will he answer by bringing Ken back into the fold? Back to us?" Martin hugged his sister-in-law with tears his own eyes.

"I'm sure He will. I'm sure your Ken isn't too far away. We've prayed for his safe arrival. Have faith." He paused and subtly continued, "Maybe God expects you to humble yourself and go back out west to Ken with a heart-felt apology for leaving him."

"Never! Ha! Fat lot of good praying for us is doing." Sherry said, and then she remembered Murray. Her next words came through a flood of tears. "Martin, look at the situation me and the boys are in. We're alone. The boys don't have a father. He smokes and drinks and swears."

Before Martin could switch to another subject, Murray did it for him.

"Please, Mommy, can we spend some time with Tadcu and Mamcu?" Murray asked.

Martin's eyebrows rose. "Tadcu and Mamcu? Where did he learn the Welsh words for grandmother and grandmother?"

"From Ken," Sherry answered, then turned back to her son. "Maybe some night we'll sleep here."

"We've been with Grandfather and Grandmother Turehue since arriving in Forest Lake," Murray said. "I want to spend some time with Tadcu and Mamcu."

"You, Murray and Kirk would be welcome," Martin said.

"Thank you, Martin," Sherry said. "I think I'd like that. That sounds like something to look forward to when the warmer weather arrives." She reached for Murray's hand. "Come home, now. Kirk is getting sleepy. It's rest time for him."

Instead of obeying his mother, the boy knelt, but he was too short for his head and arms to rest on the pew seat. He stood up and hoisted himself onto the seat. He sat still, his feet not touching the floor, his eyes closed. Sherry watched as her son sat like this for a long time not saying a word out loud, but talking to God.

Martin felt Sherry's vibrating temper subside upon seeing her young son praying so fervently. Martin knelt and soon he felt Sherry kneel beside him.

"I'm praying that Murray's Daddy will stop his smoking and drinking and cussing, and that he will stay home more with Mommy and the boys so Mommy won't cry so much. I know she cries a lot at night and when she's alone, because Murray told us so. And I'm praying for his Uncle Bradan, too. That he will also learn more godly manners."

Martin stood and set a comforting hand on his nephew's shoulder. "God has given you great wisdom, my little nephew. And I'm glad you came here."

"Thank you, Uncle Martin."

Martin wiped tears from his eyes with one hand.

"Just like He did your daddy at your age. But your Daddy will be wise again; this is just a temporary hindrance."

One evening in the first week of May, Martin helped Sherry move her and the boys' belongings to his parents' place. The house wasn't fancy, a one-story stone house on a ridge overlooking Lake Forest and Forest Lake village.

Having placed the last of the boys' clothing in dresser drawers, Sherry joined the rest of the family in the living-room.

She flopped into an easy chair, swiped flaxen-coloured hair from her eyes, and wiped her sweaty brow. Although it hadn't actually rained, clouds covered the sun, making the day hot and humid.

Murray climbed onto Mamcu's lap, whose hair streaked with silver. She rocked back and forth in her chair while Murray snuggled.

"What a day this has been," Sherry said. "I think I'll put Murray to bed early." "They do look tired," Martin agreed.

"So do you," Tadcu said, his head also bearing silver. Then the baby started to wail hungrily from his bassinet. "I'm coming, Kirk," Sherry said.

Sherry went to his bassinet, picked him up, then carried him back to her seat and prepared to nurse.

"It's nice to sleep at Grandma and Grandpa Turehue's, but I like it with Tadcu and Mamcu Asquinn," Murray said.

"Murray, I'm busy feeding your baby brother right now." Her words came out a little more sharply than she wanted.

At his downcast face, Mamcu wrapped her arms around the boy, knowing Murray had been cut deep by his mother's sharp answer.

"I understand why you are snappish with your children," she said. "This situation is new for you."

"Murray and Kirk are Ken's sons," Martin said, worried at Sherry's mood. "That makes them Asquinns as are you. So all of you are where you belong. Right here in this house."

Murray slid from his grandmother's chair and moved to stand by his mother and watched his mother and Kirk. When the baby finished his meal, Sherry placed an old towel over her shoulder, hoisted Kirk up and started patting his back. After a while with no burp, Sherry gently bounced him up and down in an effort to get him to do so. At last he burped, spewing sour-smelling milk all over the towel. Sherry took him down from her shoulder and wiped his face.

Martin cringed as Kirk started crying at the top of his lungs. Sherry hugged him and got up and walked with him, but he would not be comforted.

Sherry sighed. "Alright, then, grumpy. Bath time for you, and then bedtime."

Mamcu stood up and held out her arms for the baby. "I'll give him his bath. You have enough to tend to with Murray."

"Thanks," Sherry said and handed Kirk to her. Mamcu disappeared with Kirk into the bathroom.

Sherry turned to Murray. "Get ready for bed, and then I will listen to your prayers." "But, Mommy, I already said my prayers at the church."

Sherry reached for Murray's hand, but he jerked it away. "Murray, come along!"

Murray lay on his back on the couch and wailed.

Sherry waved her arms in the air in impatience, then glanced at Martin, embarrassed. "Sorry you have to see him acting like this."

Sherry held out her hands to Murray again. "Come on, Murray. No more of this. To bed now, and then I'll listen to your bedtime prayers."

"No. I'll go to bed, but I won't say my prayers." Sherry nodded. "Okay."

Murray finally took one of his mother's hands with his small one and she helped him to his feet. Martin and Audrey followed Sherry and Murray to the boys' bedroom, the same bedroom the boys' father had slept in as a boy.

"Get into your pyjamas and into bed, all right?" Sherry said, "I'll see if Mamcu needs help."

"Okay, Mommy."

By the time Sherry got back to the bathroom, Mamcu had dried Kirk and dressed him in fresh, sweet-smelling bedclothes. Sherry reached out for him.

"I'll put him to bed," Mamcu kindly said. "You rest. You're tired."

"Are you sure?"

"I haven't forgotten how to look after young'uns," Mamcu assured her.

Kirk continued to wail as Mamcu tried to settle him. Finally, after a little bit of rocking, he quieted and his eyes drooped shut.

Sherry picked up a laundry basket placed in one corner of the room and set it on the dresser top. She took out diapers and started to fold. When the diapers were folded, she put them away in a drawer. Martin joined her and helped her fold a basketful of Murray's clothing.

Sherry turned her hazel eyes on Martin. "What do you think, Martin? Does this room mark me a failure as a wife and mother with it being so cluttered? I remember when you, Martha and I were children your mother had kept every room clean and neat and free of dust."

She swept her hand around the room, "Look at the dirty diapers waiting for a washing machine and clean diapers, unfolded and wrinkled, scattered everywhere. I remember Martha had always kept her room clean and sparkling and everything in order, even though she had a younger sister, Faith, in the room with her."

Sherry sniffed as she continued. "I know the congregation brands me as a failure because of the breakdown of my marriage. I'm a marked woman to be pitied, and I feel this whenever I encounter a member of the church even though it wasn't me who broke my vows. I did all I could as a wife to Ken. It's him that has fallen away and abandoned us long before I moved back here."

"That's why you refuse to attend Golden Ridge Baptist Church," Martin said.

Sherry closed the dresser drawer hard and Kirk stirred, then woke with a definitely cranky wail.

"Hey, you," Sherry said. She went over to the crib, leaned over the top rail, and looked down at the baby. He pumped his legs and wailed away. Fearful he might wake Murray, Sherry scooped him up.

"Wet," she said to no one in particular. "'We'll soon have you cleaned and dry."

She pulled the entire bundle, all fluffy and fresh smelling, to her and hugged him tight.

Kirk responded with a delighted chortle.

Martin heard voices in the living room. "Dad's back," he said.

"Well, might as well put the baby back in his crib and go into the living room and face the music," Sherry said to Martin. But, when she returned Kirk to his crib he cried. Sherry scooped him back up again before he woke his brother. Her efforts were in vain. Murray woke up and followed Martin and Sherry to the front of the house. Martin sat down on the couch beside Audrey. Sherry sat at one end of the couch closest to Tadcu's chair.

"Are you and the boys comfortable?" Tadcu asked.

"Yes, thank you, Tadcu," Murray answered.

"Yes, thank you," Sherry said. "When I left the west, I was determined to manage on my own. My plan to live with my parents or in-laws was to only have been temporary. Now I'm thinking seriously of moving into the apartment in back of Dad's store. I've asked Ken for a divorce."

"You are welcome to stay here as long as you need to," Mamcu said. Martin noticed the flash of annoyance cross his father's face.

"Thank you," Sherry said.

"When I married you and Ken, it was onto a lifetime commitment," Pastor Asquinn said. "How will you support yourself?"

"Maybe Dad will let me work as a clerk in the shop," Sherry said not responding to his first comment. "I wish I'd finished school, then I could become a school teacher like Martin."

"Huh?" Martin said. He'd never realized Sherry wanted to be like him.

"We are starting a Christian school here in Forest Lake," Pastor Asquinn said. "There's lots of positions to be filled."

"I'm going back to school and finish grade twelve," Sherry said. "Martin is lucky enough to teach right here in the Forest Lake public school."

"And then what?" Pastor Asquinn asked.

Kirk squirmed in Sherry's arms and Sherry wriggled in her chair. Martin noticed Audrey growing fidgety, her hands clenching and unclenching, not knowing what to do with her hands with no baby to change or feed.

"Then I will home school Murray and Kirk," Sherry said. "It doesn't take as much teacher's training to teach in a private organization as a public school."

Mamcu reached out to take Kirk into her arms, but Audrey stepped in. "May I?"

"Certainly," Sherry said and made the transfer.

Kirk smiled up at Audrey, his smile having more power over her than a beautiful sunset. "Must have been the humidity causing those two to be cranky today," Sherry remarked.

"Those boys need their father," Tadcu said.

"I know they do, Pastor Asquinn, but Ken can't be that father right now. I'm praying that someday he will be again. Just with Ken's drinking and swearing and adulterous behaviour with a female civilian working at the police station, I didn't want that kind of example for Murray and Kirk. I'm hoping my being here will help Ken realize he needs to clean himself up and get right with God and become a husband and father again."

"Well, right now, I'd like to hold my grandson, please."

Audrey passed the baby over. As Tadcu cooed over the baby, the tension in the room vanished. He didn't cast anymore accusing looks Sherry's way; he was totally into his grandson. Sherry even laughed at something he said.

Amazing how a baby could change the atmosphere from tense to relaxing and enjoyable. "This is a good time to go home," Martin said to Audrey.

Pastor Asquinn and Mamcu accompanied the couple to the kitchen door.

"How are your adoption plans progressing?" Mamcu asked. Have you heard any more from the child welfare people?"

"Not yet," Audrey said and Martin shook his head sadly.

"Well, I'm sure you'll hear something soon. Don't be too discouraged. Good night," Mamcu said, then Pastor Asquinn repeated the farewell as the couple opened the door and stepped out into the dark night.

"Good night," Martin and Audrey called back over their shoulders.

"Look, Audrey, we have a caller," Martin said as they approached the house. Audrey glanced at her wrist watch. "At nine o'clock at night?"

"Social workers can show up any time of the day or night," Martin reminded her.

Ten minutes later, the couple and the lady stood in the kitchen. "Mrs. Moore, we will not allow them to be separated."

"I'm sorry, Mr. And Mrs. Asquinn, but there is another couple interested in adopting two of the soon-to-be-born quintuplets," Miss Moore said, "There might not be anything that can be done but comply."

"Those five will grow up together, with us," Audrey insisted. "They're a set." She sniffed and pulled a Kleenex from a box and wiped her eyes.

"We don't have children of our own, although we've been married over two years. This should give us priority consideration," Martin said.

"Five babies all at one time," Mrs. Moore said. "Are you sure you want to do this?' "We are sure," Audrey insisted. She looked at Martin.

He smiled. "Absolutely,"

"We will see what we can do about you adopting all five, but don't set your heart on it. I must hurry along to another case."

Once they were alone, Martin put an arm around Audrey's waist and drew her to him. "Martin, I am not going to allow it."

Two
Ken's Plan

Ken turned the key in the lock, and opened the door. Sometimes he wondered why he kept coming home. It wasn't home to him anymore. Not really. One of the reasons he stayed out many nights even after his shifts was because he had no desire to go home. But Sherry was expecting him to come home. Perhaps that's why he kept doing it.

He pushed open the door. He paused for one more look around at the mid-May morning.Dark clouds with white clouds piled on top. *Going to be a bad thunderstorm sometime today, he thought.* Ken stepped inside, then closed the door behind him. The silence in the house was *overwhelming*. He remained by the door, for some reason not getting his feet to respond to the command to move further into the house. All else faded out and thoughts of five months before in late January, took over his mind.

"Sherry?" He called as he kicked off his shoes. There was no answer. "Sherry, my love, where are…?" Ken called again, in Welsh. The only reply he received were the street noises outside. His mind flashed back six months. He'd just returned home from work, so he'd let Sherry think. His knees grew weak with apprehension as he walked into the bedroom. The silence throughout the house roared in his ears. The closet doors were open and his beloved's clothes were not on their hangers. Her largest suitcases were missing.

The boys!

He dashed out of the bedroom and to the boys' room. Scattered items on the floor and the emptiness of the closets told him they were gone, too.

He groaned.

He hurried back to the master bedroom, and found the picture of his and Sherry's wedding picture staring at him from the top of her dresser. He picked up the picture and gazed down at Sherry looking so young and so happy. Then he spied the note taped to the dresser mirror, he tore it off and read the words.

"My beloved Ken, by the time you read this note I will be across the prairies and into Ontario. I found out about your adulterous carryings on. You lied to me. You were not working overtime, or night shifts. You were with another. So, I'm writing to say good-bye, Ken. Don't bother to follow me. The next you hear from me will be through my lawyer about a divorce. Not that I need them because God says in his word a man or woman can divorce once a partner commits adultery. Murray, Kirk, and I will be fine.

"Most important of all, Ken, you were deeply loved. I still love you. The only way to get me back is for you to change your ways. I pray every day that God will turn you around.

"Sherry"

Ken stared at the picture.

"That stupid Bible and its hopeless, pointless words," he said. He kicked the end of the bed in anger and frustration.

"Why fight? Why not give Sherry the freedom she wants so badly. I've really tried to keep to the ways I my parents raised with, but every time I try, I end up failing. I don't have the strength to fight anymore."

Ken's mind turned to the typewriter in front of him. He'd been trying to think of a response for the last three days, but nothing would come to him. This time, for the hundredth time, he swallowed several times from the bottle, then started typing.

"My dearest Sherry,

"After reading your note, I feel that if a divorce is what you want, then a divorce you should have, and will get. Send me the papers to sign; I will not contest anything."

He paused in his typing and took several more swallows, but this time gagged on the contents. He hurried to the bathroom and spat out the liquid, then scrubbed his lips with a wet wash cloth. When he went back to his typing, his fingers did not hit the letters he wanted and his mind kept wandering from what he wanted to say. He set his elbows on the table and rested his head on his hands, then wiped his face with one hand.

What's the matter with me? I'm not so drunk I can't type a letter? He tried again.

"You can have custody of the boys, which is why I'm writing you; I won't have any more say in the way they are raised. I know you won't be happy having them raised in any other way but attending every kind of church service and camp there is. You, and everyone in the church there at Forest Lake, will see that the boys are brought up in strong Bible doctrine. I'm not the kind of father you want for our sons, as I am too ungodly to give them this. So, it is good-bye, my lovely Charlotte. Forget about me entirely, and don't so much as mention me in your prayers.

With that said, you won't hear from me again except through my lawyer. "*Your loving husband, Ken."*

Ken wiped tears from his eyes, then swallowed again and again from his bottle. With shaking hands, he addressed the envelope, folded the letter and slid it inside. Then he sealed the envelope and put a stamp on it.

He was in the entrance way on his way to drop the letter in the mailbox on the corner.

A noise brought his mind back to the entrance way. He looked behind him to see that Gwen had come into the room wrapped in a bathrobe, her hair covered in a thick, soft towel.

Instead of mailing the letter, he turned and went back to the bedroom. Ken turned his attention back to the pictures.

He studied the pictures of his wife, both of them so happy after their betrothal, some more recent after their marriage, of the children. Sherry always looked at him, love glowing on her face and in her eyes. He quaked so much he couldn't take a step. He sank slowly to the floor. He sat, arms wrapped around his legs and face buried in his knees.

"What's the matter with you?" Gwen asked. "Still drunk, I suppose.

Why don't you forget about your wife? She left you. Have a good time now."

Ken moaned in agony. "You don't care! You're disgusted with me right now. There isn't an ounce of sympathy in you for me. There never was. All you ever wanted from our relationship was a good time. You never did care what happened to me. I could use some of my sweet wife's genuine love right now. I know I have not had enough to drink so I can't even stand up and walk. Is this what alcohol has done to me? Is this the results of the last ten years?"

Ken lifted his eyes heavenward. "I remember that summer when Bradan, Sherry, Martha and I got stranded on that reef. I ought to consider myself lucky. You could easily have killed me, but instead you granted me life and favor so that I could live for you. I realized that only this moment.

Ken paused. He felt a real presence beside him—invisible but there. "I know it's you intervening, Lord, to save Charlotte and my marriage. I know we are not as close we were when I was a kid. But, I want to know your will for my life. I want to get back to that wonderful relationship we once had."

Through the porch door he could see all the way into the kitchen and the dreadful liquor bottle on the table. He saw the bottle and its contents through different eyes now. It was a long time before he attempted to get back on his feet. When he did, he went through to the kitchen, put the envelope containing his letter in the back pocket of his jeans, picked up the bottle and went down into the basement.

Ken switched on the ceiling lights. A bright, cheerful, yellow glow filled the basement room. The area had been finished with bright birch panelling on the walls, and plywood floors with linoleum on top.

Ken went to his liquor cupboard. Two by two, one in each hand, he lifted out the bottles and set them on the counter. One remained in his hand and he paused for a moment, stared at the ever so colourful bottle and the ever-changing colours of the liquid inside.

Gwen had followed him around and into the basement.

"What are you doing? Who are you talking to?" she snarled. "You've lost your senses. It's from all that liquor you consume."

"I'm sober and have just come to my senses," Ken told her. "I don't expect you to understand." He continued his conversation with his

Maker as he proceeded to rid his life of the evil that had dragged him down. He didn't stop until every last drop had drained away and out of his life. Whistling a tune from one of the old-time hymns he had known as a child, he went back upstairs, ripped up the letter he'd written to his wife, envelope and all, cleaned up and started another letter.

When he'd finished the letter, he turned to Gwen. "Gwen, get dressed."

"What?" Gwen choked. She looked at Ken, not grasping what he was saying at all. "I'm going back to Ontario and reconcile with my wife," Ken said.

Gwen stared at Ken for a few seconds, then, without a word, when she realized he was serious, whirled on her heels and left the room. Ken heard her dialling on the phone and ask for a cab.

Fifteen minutes later the doorbell rang. He heard the door open then slam shut. Ken went to the front door and peeked out the window just as a taxi backed out of his driveway and turned to go elsewhere.

Ken went to bed that night, sober and alone, but he could not sleep. He tossed and turned, as he kept thinking about the miles to span that separated him from his beloved Sherry. Giving up on sleep, he got up. He pulled on his jeans, socks and a shirt, pushed his feet into comfortable casual shoes. He loaded only a few toiletries, his musical instruments which, even after all these years, he could never leave behind, and every family picture in the house. In the coolness of the early morning and the light from the street lamp, he backed his light green-coloured 1966 Chevy 2 car out onto the street and started the long journey towards home. He literally drove away from all that he had accumulated—his job, his home and worldly possessions. He was ready to start his journey back to Forest Lake and reclaim his reason for existence.

Out on the open highway at last, he turned the car east and started the journey back to familiarity and freedom. Freedom from his slavery to drink, smoking, adultery and all his other sins and into the future of his glorious promised land – a life with his beloved Charlotte. That's all that mattered to him now.

He had driven a lot of hours even before the sun started to show above the endless prairie fields. In Fort William/Port Arthur, he stopped to gas up the car, and then drove as fast as he safely could for the insistent urging to get home and be reunited with his family had overcome him.

And as he drove, he prayed.

"Father in Heaven, please make this long trip home and leaving all behind worthwhile. I ask that you will change Sherry's heart so that she will take me back. Amen."

He stepped on the gas, but, before he could increase his speed too much, a police siren wailed behind him. Ken glanced at the rear-view mirror. He slammed his palms against the steering wheel and pulled over. He had composed himself by the time the Ontario Provincial Police officer stopped at his window.

"Sir," the officer greeted with a touch of the brim of his hat. "Sir." Ken returned the greeting and gesture.

"May I see some identification?"

Ken fished in his back jeans pocket and brought out his wallet. He opened the brown leather case, separated some documents and handed them to the officer.

"My registration and driver's license."

The officer took them and looked the papers over. "What are you doing in Ontario?"

"I was raised in Ontario."

"Your car is loaded to the hilt with instruments."

"I'm going back to where I grew up to get my wife back. Couldn't leave the instruments behind."

The officer had nothing to say to that. He straightened and again touched the brim of his hat.

"I wish you luck in getting your wife back. And watch your speed; you won't be any good to your wife dead or mangled. Take an extra hour or two and arrive in one piece."

"Yes, sir, good advice. I will."

"Officer," Ken called after the policeman had gone a step or two. The officer returned to the window. "Is it true the provincial police are short of good men?"

"Oh, yes. Especially in towns off the beaten path. But why would you be interested?" "Where does one recruit?" Ken asked without answering the officer's question.

The officer tore a page from his notebook, wrote on it and handed the paper to him. "Thank you, sir." Ken waved as he drove off this time at a reasonable rate of speed. As Ken drove, he suddenly felt physically stronger. His only desire was to get home to his own family. He knew others, and he hoped this included his adored Sherry, were praying at that very moment.

What would he find at the end of his long journey across three provinces, after driving more than 2000 miles?

Three
Living in Harmony

The dream started again.

Taffy, the beautiful Arabian mare, reared with the teen-age girl in the saddle. Ken parked on the highway that ran parallel with the field the trial riders were crossing and honked the horn. Ken, Bradan, and Martin didn't notice the truck approach then pass. There was a loud clattering noise as the truck hit a pothole and a loose fishing tackle box tipped over in the truck bed spilling its contents. Everyone watched in horror as the mare reared, whinnied, flailed her front legs and screamed as she went over backwards. She landed right on her rider.

Bradan felt movement beside him. He turned his head and opened his eyes and slowly a woman's face focused.

The woman put a hand on his shoulder. "Having another nightmare about that horse, Bradan?"

"Yeah, Martha, I sure am." Bradan searched for the face of the clock on the bedside table with blurred vision. "Five A.M."

He turned on his side, and reached out and pulled Martha towards him. She willingly fell into his arms.

"You sure are frisky for coming in after midnight off your shift," Martha teased.

Martha closed her eyes as Bradan's lips covered hers. Her arms tightened around him and her lips sought his. His eyes looked sad when he released her.

"What's the matter, my handsome husband?" Martha asked.

"It's nothing, really."

"Come on. Something's bothering you."

"I received orders yesterday. I'm being transferred to the Yukon Territory." "And that bothers you?"

"Not me, but I thought it might bother you."

"Moving doesn't bother me at all," Martha said.

"I'm glad to hear that," Bradan said and kissed her. "We'll prepare to move immediately." "I will," Martha assured her husband. She pushed back the covers and set her legs over the edge of the bed.

"Well, since I'm awake, I might as well check on the boys."

Bradan moaned, turned over and was soon fast asleep.

The room was bright with sunlight when Bradan next awoke. The bedside clock said, "1:00".

Bradan pushed back the covers. He dressed and joined Martha who was already in the kitchen.

"Where are Gerald and Lyle?" he asked.

"The boys are in the living-room," Martha said.

Bradan continued into the living room where he picked up his youngest son and cuddled him. Gerald looked on, waiting for his turn. Bradan set Lyle down. There was a lot of laughing and gales of laughter as Bradan lifted Gerald up and swung him around until both were good and tired.

"Lunch?" Martha asked.

"I'm starving," Bradan said.

Later that evening, as the sun began to lose some of its heat, Bradan and Martha were in the kitchen at the table.

Martha set her cup of coffee on the saucer in front of her. Bradan sipped his coffee and then replaced the mug on the table. The family had eaten, and Gerald and Lyle were in bed.

"I'm starting my four days off and I haven't seen Ken for such a long time," Bradan said. "I'm going to telephone him and invite him here for a visit. Maybe he will have some idea of something exciting to do."

He strode into the front room, reached for the telephone and dialled Ken's number. It rang and rang. No answer.

Bradan looked puzzled. "I'll dial again. Maybe I dialled wrong."

"Did you say something, dear?" Martha asked from the kitchen.

"No, darling," Bradan replied, then dialled again.

Again, no answer. "Odd," Bradan said.

He returned the receiver to its place, and sat back in the easy chair. "You look worried. Is something wrong, darling?" Martha said.

"I have a terrible feeling something is dreadfully wrong. Ken didn't answer."

"That reminds me. A letter came for you this morning." She pulled an envelope from her apron pocket and handed it to him. Bradan took the envelope eagerly, but his face drained of colour after reading the return address.

"It's from Ken."

He paused and stared at the envelope. "Beth sy'd digwydd?" Martha demanded.

"What? What did you say? You and Ken have that annoying habit of talking Welsh and I can't understand what you're saying."

Martha smiled in spite of his obvious frustration.

"Sorry, Bradan. What is going on? Why don't you open the envelope and read the letter, dear?"

Bradan continued to hold the unopened letter in both hands. "I have a very bad feeling about this."

He glanced at the stamp on the upper right corner. "This letter was mailed a week ago on May the fifteenth, in Saskatchewan."

Martha handed him the letter opener. Carefully, Bradan slid the sharp edge along the top of the envelope, then slowly drew the neatly folded letter out, unfolded it.

"My dear friend, Bradan,

Why am I writing to you? ...Let me see. Where to start? I'm leaving the RCMP...

"By the time you get this letter, I will be well on my way to Forest Lake. Sherry left me and I'm going to win her back. I pray my efforts will be successful and I have every reason to believe He has heard my prayers. She sounded serious in the note she left me asking for a divorce. Apparently she's

found out about my extra duty activities."

Bradan cleared his throat and let the last sentence trail off and began on the next paragraph.

"Oh my," Martha said. "I feel so sad for both of them." Bradan continued reading.

"When I first read her note I was inclined to agree with her and give her the divorce she wants so badly. I even tried writing her a note letting her know I'd agreed. However, this was one letter God made sure did not get written.

"I've simply walked away from the Mounties. I didn't like the force's brutal ways and was planning to quit anyway. I feel strongly God intends for me to go after Sherry and win her back. I'm only sorry I had to leave you, Martha and my little nephews out of my plans. I hoped you would have been able to accompany me and we all would have returned to Forest Lake, then you and I could have joined the Ontario Provincial Police together. We both would be much happier with them. Bradan, I know you are not happy where you are; neither was I happy where I was.

"I will write you more when I get settled in Forest Lake with Sherry, Murray and Kirk. Furthermore, I will inquire about a place for you on our own police force if you are interested. Please write and let me know if you would be interested in an offer like this."

Ken signed off in Welsh. Bradan couldn't read the language so she handed the letter to Martha who read out loud, in English:

"Martha, Lots of love

Bradan, so long. I hope this isn't good-bye, and best wishes. Your friend,

Ken."

Martha handed the pages back to Bradan. Bradan set the letter aside. He was having a difficult time holding back a flood of tears.

"Why didn't he phone and let us know what's going on? I would have walked away from this terrible job I have now and gone back with him; then he wouldn't be alone. Who's going to make sure he gets back to Forest Lake in one piece?"

Martha reached out and touched Bradan's arm.

"Darling, I don't believe Ken is alone. For the first time in many years it sounds like he's following God's directing."

Bradan glared at her.

"My brother didn't escape God's wrath this time."

"What are you talking about?" Bradan said sharply.

"That night the four of us were stranded on that reef. Sherry and I believe that God sent that storm to punish Ken for losing the tithing money. Martha and I turned away the storm by asking God to do so. Now Sherry's left him. We should be praying for him."

Bradan sprang to his feet. "What foolishness you talk. He will get home safely. What does the night on the reef have to do with our lives now?"

"Bradan, please don't go out," Martha said, instead of answering Bradan's question. "It's getting late. You need your rest."

"I don't need you to tell me when I need my rest."

"Oh, my darling Bradan, all I'm trying to tell you....."

Her words trailed off as she caught sight of Gerald on the staircase. Gerald dashed down the remaining stairs and grabbed the leg of his father's trousers.

"Don't go, Daddy, please."

"Where will you go?" Martha asked.

Bradan waved his arms as saying he had no idea where to go or what to do next before letting the door slam shut behind him.

A thunderous silence followed. Martha picked up Gerald, squeezed him tight, and leaned against the sink. A noise came from a different part of the house. Martha started and put a hand over her heart.

Perhaps Lyle fell out of his crib. But then there would have been crying. "Spooky," she said to Gerald.

"Spooky, Mommy," Gerald said.

"Where did that noise come from?" She started towards the staircase upstairs, Gerald behind her. She'd set one foot on the bottom step when the noise came, again, sharp and loud. It startled Martha so much her heart pounded. She grabbed the staircase for support. But, the noise didn't seem to come from upstairs this time. She changed direction and walked cautiously towards the living-room.

She sighed in relief when loud crashing sounds like someone one playing the cymbals reached her.

"Oh, the car stereo."

She bowed her head right where she was. Dear God, Martha prayed, *please don't allow my husband to reach any drinking establishment this evening. I feel strongly if he consumes liquor this evening this will be the end of any hope of restoration with you. Please stop him and bring him back home to his family where he belongs. Only you will know how to do this.*

Martha opened her eyes. She listened for the sound of Bradan starting the vehicle's engine, but there was only silence. She went back to the kitchen window. With Gerald in her arms, she watched Bradan open the car door, get in behind the wheel, and start the engine. For a reason she could not explain, he appeared to have no desire to back out into the street. He just sat in his car. Martha wondered what he was thinking about. After a few seconds he turned the engine off.

Martha's sympathy went out to her husband. He looked discouraged, defeated, and not knowing where, or to whom to turn. He rested his arms on the steering wheel and buried his face in them. He did not look up for a long time as he wrestled with his Maker.

Then, finally, when he did look up, it was to the heavens. Martha didn't mean to eavesdrop on her husband, but the window was open.

"I realize I have been really stupid in the way I've lived my life the past few years," he confessed. "I've known all along there is no other but your way, yet I wanted to live and conduct my life the way I thought it should be. I've done nothing but meet with one disaster after another. I plead with you to restore me back to the fellowship with you I once knew—no, if it pleases you, put me on an even higher level. I want to know your will in my life."

Bradan remained seated in the car for some time after that.

Martha said to Gerald, "Bed for you."

"Yes, Mommy," Gerald answered sleepily.

Martha set him down and the little boy dashed for his room.

From her vantage point, thrills ran through Martha as she watched peace flood through her husband, a peace she knew he had not experienced since he was a boy. She knew he walked again with the Lord.

Martha turned and went upstairs to tuck the boys in. She had just finished tucking a blanket around Gerald when she heard Bradan come in. She dashed down the stairs where she held out her arms in joyful welcome.

Bradan held her close and kissed her. "I guess you were watching."

"Yes, my dear Bradan. I saw and heard everything."

"The boys are in bed, right?"

"Yes, they are."

After several more delicious kisses—Martha couldn't remember such kisses—Bradan picked her up and carried her in his arms towards the bedroom.

"I'm sorry I was cross with you," Bradan said later. "I don't know why I get so short tempered with you. I realize you only want what's best for me. I hope you are praying for Ken and Sherry, my precious one."

Martha turned over to face him. He lay on his back staring up at the ceiling. "Why, Bradan my beloved, yes, I am," Martha replied in her native Cumraig.

Bradan was used to his wife breaking into her native language. He even partially understood what Martha had just said.

"I know Sherry has every right to do what she's doing but I'm praying she will show her husband mercy and forgiveness and take him back."

"Good," Bradan said. There was no mockery in his voice this time. "Keep on. I'm certain God will answer your prayers. Judging by the tone of Ken's letter, that man is very hurt. I'm sorry I can't be there for him."

"Maybe it is God's will you aren't. Don't you think it is time for Ken and Sherry learn to be there for each other?"

Bradan thought this over carefully. "Hmm. I think you are right, my precious one." He thought some more, then continued sadly, "I'm not sure I know how to pray anymore. I'm afraid God won't even hear and answer; not after the way I've behaved and cursed His name over the past few years."

Martha reached out and rested a hand on Bradan's knee. Love washed through him at the contact and his body responded.

"Simply pray the way you used to when your belief was stronger."

"But prayer is to be tempered with faith. I don't have that kinda conviction anymore."

"Yes you do, Bradan. It's just Satan trying to con you into believing otherwise so you

won't have the power of God at your disposal to use against him." Bradan fell silent. Martha glanced at him.

"Why don't we both pray for Ken and Sherry right now?" she suggested. Bradan glanced at her. "You mean, there's power in numbers?"

"No, silly. But God does love to hear united prayer from families, and husbands and wives."

"I know you're right."

There was a minute or two of silence then Bradan said with strong determination. "We will say a prayer for that couple right here and now."

Bradan and Martha got out of bed, and wrapped in night robes, knelt by the side of the bed.

Before closing his eyes, Bradan noticed that Gerry had opened the adjoining door and had been about to enter their room. He was dressed in his pyjamas. He stopped when he saw Mommy and Daddy bowed in an attitude of prayer.

"Come and join us, Ger. It's time this family learned to pray together." Gerry went further into the bedroom and joined his parents by the bedside.

"Our Father in Heaven," Bradan began. "It is heartbreaking to see my best friend's marriage come to such a fate as it has. Maybe he deserves it, no, I know he does. But you have the power to overturn circumstances and restore broken homes. I know I haven't been consistent in prayer to you and seeking your will, or showing you any love over the past few years; but now I come before you on my knees to ask that you show mercy to my friend, Ken. Please put in it Sherry's heart to forgive him and take him back.

"Thy will be done. "Amen."

Bradan noticed a happier look on Gerry's face as he went back to his room. Bradan was happier too as he was certain he and Martha were now living in harmony. They'd been united in prayer.

"Thank you for the kind prayer for my brother," Martha said as she and Bradan straightened up. Martha caught the glint of tears in his eyes.

"I wish I could do more for him. I feel so helpless."

"It is enough," Martha reassured him. "Just leave our prayers at Jesus' feet and we will be astonished at the results."

"How many nights have I excluded myself from these family prayer sessions?" Bradan said.

"Lots. If we prayed more together our two families might not have gone through so many difficulties. At least, if we were united in God it would have been easier."

"This could have been one night in many should have prayed together as a family. Instead this is the first ever, I'm embarrassed to admit. We will pray like this every night for Ken to reach Forest Lake safely."

"And for Sherry to forgive him and take him back," Martha said.

"That too. I intend to do this every night for as long as you and I are together on this earth. I haven't felt such peace in a long time. This is what this marriage has lacked—strong husbandly spiritual leadership. I feel that all will be well between Ken and Sherry."

Bradan cupped Martha's face in his hands and turned her head until she looked directly at him. "How are you standing up to this? First about our move, and what this means for Gerry and Lyle, then the news about Ken and Sherry."

"I'm doing fine. I don't know how our sons are taking all this."

Bradan released her. The two of them remained seated on the edge of the bed. "What are you going to do, Bradan? Will you quit the Mounties also and go back to Ontario?"

"Maybe not right away, but I will contact the police in Ontario and fill out an application," Bradan said with determination, knowing that what he would do with the rest of his life was etched on his mind.

Four
Full Circle

Ken sat in the visitor's chair in the Lakeview detachment of the Ontario Provincial Police force across the desk from the recruiting officer.

"Show me where to sign," Ken said.

The officer set an application form and pen on the desk. "If you would just sign here, sir."

Ken took the pen and swiftly filled out the form and signed.

"Someone will get in touch with you over the next few weeks and let you know when you can start."

Ken left the office.

Leaving Lakeview, Ken steered his car towards the route that would take him to Highway 11, and then north twenty-one more miles before he could see his Sherry.

Twenty minutes later, Ken came to the spot along the highway where the Arctic Watershed sign stood. He pulled over into this wide spot and parked. This was the spot where he and Sherry and Bradan and Martha stopped for last words before starting their honeymoons so many years before. Four more miles and he would be home and with his loved one once again.

Ken got out of the car and strode towards a patch of wildflowers and started picking.

When he'd finished, Ken had a bouquet of purple Swamp Loosestrife, white Aster, Blue Ragged

Fringed Orchid, and green and brown Large Round leaf orchid. Looking around, he spied a shady wooded area and started in that direction. He saw white blooms growing all over the forest floor. He squatted and with one hand carefully reached for a flower and picked it ever so tenderly. Then he returned to his car and set the bouquet on the passenger seat.

Slowly Ken drove along the main thoroughfare through Forest Lake.

"Forest Lake! What a sight! What a change. This used to be a gravel road, now it's paved," Ken said in Welsh since there was no one around to complain.

He rolled down his window and found comfort in the many sweet scents that drifted to his nostrils on a strong breeze: the grass, the lake, pine, spruce, poplar, birch, and countless flowers.

Ken slowed and turned into the driveway to the familiar stone house on the ridge, which also had been paved. He parked in the family lot off to one side at the front, got out and walked alongside the house to the back porch and the entrance. He walked through the porch and into the kitchen closing the door softly. On light feet he moved to the living-room door and paused to peek inside. Family sat in various seats, the couch and easy chairs. His father sat in an easy chair, an open Bible on his lap. Family worship time. Ken was about to step into the living-room and join the circle, but he heard voices at the end of the hallway and traced them to the bedroom he and Martin had shared as youths.

Through the open bedroom door, he saw Martin sitting on the bed, facing the door.

Martin held Kirk in his arms while Murray snuggled up to him.

Sherry sat with her back to the door at a student desk. The very desk he used while in high school. What looked like textbooks were open in front of her, and she held a pencil in one hand as she wrote in a notebook. Martin said something and Sherry's chime-like laughter reached Ken's ears. Laughter, yes, but Ken did not miss the movement of Sherry's hand as she lifted it to her face and wiped away tears. She looked close to tears.

Martin smiled at Sherry. "Your laughter is beautiful. It's so nice to hear you laugh."

Ken winced. When was the last time he made Sherry want to laugh? He sniffed back tears, remembering.

Martin heard and looked up startled.

"Who could that be?" Martin said as he stood and turned towards the door. He stopped and stared at Ken standing in the doorway.

Ken moved closer to his brother and whispered in his ear and said, politely, without the attitude the family had last heard from him. "I wish to talk to my wife, alone."

"Sure thing," Martin said.

Ken waved a hand, indicating that Martin was to follow him into the hall. Both brothers were relaxed in the others presence.

"There's a bedroom under construction just off the kitchen. It used to be part of the porch," Martin whispered.

Ken nodded. "I remember."

"Sherry uses that room, and the boys use the bedroom."

"That will do fine. Thanks."

"I wish you well as you talk to Sherry, Ken," Martin said.

"Thank you."

Martin continued down the hall. From the shuffling and hushed voices in the living-room behind him, Ken knew that the family was clearing out so he and Sherry could be alone.

Ken watched from the hallway as Sherry finished with her writing and set the book aside. "Murray, I will hear your prayers now."

After saying his prayers, Murray climbed onto the bed himself. He sat on the top of the covers with his legs crossed, facing the door, not saying a word for a long time, but talking to God.

Ken was glad that Murray hadn't seen him yet because he wanted to listen.

Ken watched as Sherry placed her hand on Murray's shoulder and the child moved a bit to make room for her. She sat on the side of the bed, her back to the door.

"What are you doing, little man?"

"I'm praying for Daddy. And you too, Mommy. You both need a lot of prayer." "We sure do," Sherry agreed.

"And we will never give up hope for Daddy or Uncle Bradan."

"Do you wish for Daddy to come and get us?"

"Yes, I do," Sherry said.

"Would you go back home?" Murray continued. Sherry nodded.

"Do you love Daddy?"

"Your Daddy is God's gift to me," Sherry said. "And to you and your baby brother. Yes, I love him."

Ken stepped into the bedroom.

Murray pointed a finger, and Kirk cooed and giggled, his brown eyes focused on something out of Sherry's line of vision.

"Mommy, look!" Murray cried. "What?" Sherry said. "Daddy!"

"Murray, don't tease Mommy like this," Sherry said. Still seated on the bed, she turned her head, and gasped. "Oh, my!!"

Ken moved towards Sherry as she leapt to her feet and gathered her in his arms and kissed her.

"Thank you ever so much for those kind words, Mai Charlotte hardd." He released her.

"I'm so sorry for the way I've treated you." He handed her the fragrant bouquet of flowers. "These are for you, Charlotte, my darling." He kissed her again.

Sherry stood on her tiptoes and returned her husband's kiss then turned her attention to the bouquet of flowers. Her eyes grew wide in admiration.

"Darling, the flowers are beautiful. The smell is heavenly. Ken, you are so thoughtful. I will put them in water straight away."

Ken held out the marvelous white flower. Sherry gasped when she saw it. "For you."

"My favourite. White Trillium," Sherry cooed. Before she could take the blossom from him, Ken reached out, smoothed her rich, honey-coloured hair with one hand, and set the stem of the flower in her hair where, he thought, it sat like a crown.

"The white Trillium symbolizes harmony and dignity," Ken explained. "I pray that I will see both in this family. In the future, I visualize us with five sons."

Sherry threw her arms around her husband and kissed him. "So do I."

Sherry was about to end the embrace and kiss, but Ken drew her closer. His lips sought hers and the two kissed again before Ken walked over to Kirk's crib, picked him up and held him closely to his breast. He kissed the baby's forehead; Kirk responded with a sweet smile at his Daddy and happy, contented gurgling sounds.

"I missed you, Daddy," Murray said.

"I missed you too, son." Ken set the baby down and picked up his oldest son who nearly choked him as Murray's arms squeezed around his neck.

"I'm glad you are here," Murray said. "So am I," Ken said.

Sherry gazed lovingly into her husband's eyes. "So am I."

Ken said. "I haven't felt such peace in a long time. I want to reconnect with my family right now and I know all will be well."

"And so do I." The corners of her eyes were moist and she wiped away her tears with the palm of her hand.

Ken set Murray on the bed and turned back to Sherry and kissed her tenderly.

"Charlotte my beautiful one," Ken said in Welsh, "my little Sunbeam, I believe that is the root of all my difficulties. I've neglected leading my household spiritually, leaving the door wide open for Satan to enter and take over the way he did. I'm to blame for my afflictions and I've come to set my household in order. It's time I did that."

Ken looked at his son. "God has answered your prayers for me concerning giving up my bad habits. He saw to that before I left the west."

Sherry snuggled closer. "I thought so. I could immediately see the change in you." "It is bedtime for you, Murray," Sherry said as he released her.

Murray waited to be tucked in. Ken bent over him and kissed him. "Good night, Daddy."

"Good night, son. I love you."

Murray wiped tears from his eyes with the sleeve of his pyjamas. "I'm happy you've found us. I want to go home."

Ken reached out and ruffled the boy's hair. "I need to talk to your mother. We have lots to talk about."

"That we do," Sherry said.

"Then can we go home?" Murray said.

Ken glanced at Sherry. "We'll see. For now, you just get to sleep. Mommy and I will figure that all out."

The boy's eyelids drooped shut as Ken followed Sherry into the kitchen where she took down a vase from a cupboard, filled it with water, and arranged the flowers inside.

"What a tender touch, Ken."

Ken guided her ahead of him towards the bedroom Martin had spoken of. When he saw the area, he whistled in admiration.

"A bedroom. It's more like a suite. A couch and bed, both." "Now we can talk," Sherry said.

Sherry sat on the couch. She picked up a cushion from the arm of the couch, then set it back in place. She did this once, twice, thrice.

"I hope you aren't afraid of me," Ken said.

"More like I don't know what to expect," Sherry answered.

Ken looked directly at her. He reached for her hand, but then pulled away.

"I never imagined things would become so awkward. Are we strangers that we don't know what to do or say to each other?"

Sherry shook her head.

Finally, he couldn't resist holding her any longer and took her in his arms. Sherry's lips found his and she kissed him, her longing for him showed plainly.

Suddenly, Sherry couldn't contain her emotions anymore and buried her face in Ken's shirt.

She soon found herself pushed back against the couch cushions. He put his arms around her pulled her towards him and hugged her tightly.

"Kiss me, Sherry. Please." There was pleading and longing in his words. Sherry glanced at the door.

"There's no one else around and even if there were, we are of age and married. Come on, kiss me."

He gazed down at her, thanking God for allowing him the love of such a delightful creature. Bending his head, he covered her lips ever so gently with his mouth; feeling the softness of her lips and the moisture of her mouth, his senses stir within him.

Sherry relaxed and he felt the love and strength flowing from him to her and back to him.

Sherry felt better at this point in her life than she ever had. Strength washed through her.

Sherry threw her arms around Ken and hugged him tightly. She kissed him on the lips, then both lost all senses and their kisses were everywhere. Ken stood up and taking Sherry in his arms, carried her to the bed and set her down. He lay down on the bed beside her and the kissing continued.

"I do love you, Ken," Sherry said.

More talking was impossible as their kisses and hugs grew more intense.

"Oh, that makes me feel so good! My love for you is almost more than I can stand," Ken said. "I've always received renewed strength and assurance from you, my sunbeam."

Ken kissed her on the lips, then unbuttoned her blouse and slid it off her shoulders. When the romancing concluded, the two up and dressed.

"Now tell me after that that you want me to turn around and leave and that you never want to see my miserable hide again. I will leave if that's what you want. All I'm asking is that you make sure that is what you want. I can assure you once I'm gone I will never bother you again."

Sherry shook her head because she was too breathless to form words. "That's not what I want," she managed.

She glanced up into his face and waves of thrills swept over her as she saw the love as he gazed down at her.

"I love you, Ken," she whispered and another brief kiss followed. "I'm almost certain, after what I felt inside me, just now, we can expect Brian in nine months."

Ken reached out and grabbed Sherry by the shoulder, turned her to face him, and looked into her face.

"Brian?"

"Sure," Sherry said, a broad, blessed grin on her face. "I'm certain we can expect the third son in nine months, January."

Ken looked stunned until the full meaning of her words sunk in. He took one of Sherry's hands in his and kissed it.

"Are you sure?" "I'm certain of it."

"Yes," Sherry answered innocently. "You expect me to believe that?"

"You and I have just conceived another baby, Ken."

Sherry glowed with the knowledge she tried so desperately to convey to her spouse. Ken stood rigid for a long time.

Sherry began to feel uncomfortable, then afraid. She could feel sadness in her heart and her face crumbled, tears formed in her eyes and she lowered her head. She braced herself for rejection.

"You expect me to believe the baby is mine?" Ken said. "It is," Sherry sniffed. "Please believe me, Ken."

"Believe you? How can I do that after watching for several minutes from the hall what went on in here? Martin seemed very willing to offer his assistance."

"He is," Sherry agreed. "I've leaned on him since arriving here. I've had no one else to turn to."

"And he just happened to be," Ken said.

"Yes," Sherry answered. "I'm in the process of finishing my high school, then I will study to be a teacher at the Community College in Lakeview. Martin sometimes helps me with my homework and drives me to and from class. Sometimes he even takes me for refreshments at a restaurant after class, but he has never touched me physically. Did you see him touch me?"

'No,"Ken admitted.He smiled.Ken's smile thrilled Sherry to her toes when she was a teen-ager. It had the same affect on her now.

"Then, I don't need to fear you are falling in love with him?" Ken said.

Tears appeared in the corners of Sherry's once again. Embarrassed, she wiped them away. "No, silly. Ken, it's you I love. It's you I want."

With a whoop of joy, he swooped Sherry up in his arms and twirled her around. "Why, darling, that's wonderful, you being pregnant. And Brian is a terrific name."

Sherry laughed.

But when Ken set her down on the bed again Sherry's heart ached for Ken "Okay, now let's get down to business. I need you to listen to me," Ken said. "I'm listening."

"What did you hear about my infidelities?"

"I heard a lot while sitting and having my hair done at the hairdresser's," Sherry said. "What did you hear?" Ken asked again.

"One of the ladies said a friend of hers lives right next door to a lady that works at the police station and you were frequently seen arriving home with her. No one seemed to see you leaving."

"And you take this lady's word?"

"Not just her word, Ken. A couple from the church the boys and I attended also live close by. I should have just come out and asked you outright. I was just so angry and disappointed and hurt that you had broken our marriage covenant."

"There might be some truth amongst a lot of falsehood," Ken admitted. "I must confess after losing a friend like Dennis Owens, I was very unhappy. I should have come straight home to your comfort and understanding after telling Mrs. Owens about her husband's death. I did not go to the bar to pick up a girl and then party all night. I intended to leave after just a few drinks. I should have had enough strength and will power to resist her when she enticed me with fluttering eyelids and flattering words to be with her, time after time. I'm sorry to admit this, Sherry, and I'm ashamed of myself." Ken shook his head to clear his mind of these memories. "This happened every evening for a while after that," he said, red faced. He could not look Sherry in the eyes. He got down on his knees, folded his hands and looked straight at Sherry. "There's more. I feel I have to tell you it all in order to be truly free of the guilt and nightmares it causes me. This wasn't the first time. It goes way back to before we were even married."

Sherry remained silent for a long time and Ken saw the pain in those trusting hazel eyes. "I know I have hurt you horrifically, and I know I don't deserve it, but please forgive me."

Sherry didn't say anything for a while. Not that Ken could blame her. She broke away from his embrace and sat as far away from him as she could manage. The silence between them lasted a long time. She stood up and started towards the door, but didn't leave.

Yes, he had done wrong and broken their marital covenant and her trust far worse than she probably ever imagined. But here he was asking for her forgiveness and he hoped she saw a genuine sorrow and the aching for his family to be whole again in his eyes and on every inch of his face. He knew she longed for the same thing.

She moved closer to him. "Are you sure it's over?"

"I've given up my wicked ways and now look to Sovereign God for direction. Did you think for a moment that I would heed your request not to follow?"

"I thought you would, but I'm glad you didn't," Sherry said. "I could see God's light shining through the moment I saw you."

"He's directed me to leave the RCMP and seek reconciliation with you."

"What?" Sherry said in astonishment. "You work so fast it's hard to keep up with you at times. You went out to Regina to train there and you show up here with the Ontario Provincial Police. You never were the kind of man to let an opportunity slip through your fingers."

"I don't want you to take me back just because you feel sorry for the boys, or me. I want us to get back together again because you love me. I know I said awhile back that I'd leave if that's what you want, but know this, I haven't come all this way to beg you to take me back, I've come to claim my family, and to live in the future as a family. I'm asking you to forgive me my transgressions and move on."

Sherry moved still closer to him she whispered into his ear, "I forgive you. And I love you. Didn't my body just now convince you of that?"

The hugging started again.

"We are all human and we humans, even us Christians, sometimes stumble. I still love you and will not desert you now."

"Oh, darling, I knew I could count on God's forgiveness in your heart. Thank God for a Christian wife. I wouldn't know how to continue living on my own. I want a smile from you."

Sherry smiled so sweetly at him he kissed her again. "Now I can take my family home."

"Are you taking us back out west?"

Ken grinned. "No. My job out west doesn't exist. I am now part of the 'boys in blue'."

They laughed again. Sherry hadn't really laughed in a long time, and laughter made her feel so good.

"You are beautiful when you laugh, Sherry. You, my beautiful Charlotte, my sunbeam, are the only woman I've ever really wanted. Please believe that, my love."

Ken's use of the word "sunbeam" as a pet name for her sent a thrill rocketing through Sherry's body. It had been like this while growing up.

Sherry nodded. "I know. I acknowledge that."

"I did not want our marriage to take the direction it did, or my life to take the turn it did," Ken said sadly. "When I married you, I wanted our life to be filled with blessings and love like Mom and Dad's, like your parents."

"I know," Sherry assured him. "And it still can be that way."

"You know, I haven't had a drink since I left the west. And with God's help I will continue to leave that stuff alone."

"And I'm going to help you. So, here's what else is in store for you." She hugged and kissed him.

A door opened and closed elsewhere in house, and voices drifted in from the front of the house.

"The family is back," Sherry said.

"I will have to face Dad sooner or later," Ken said, "but not tonight. I'm exhausted from my long trip and want some rest."

The rest of the family must have realized this, because gradually the muffled sounds ceased, and silence settled over the house.

Mid-morning the next day, Ken prepared himself, rather reluctantly, to leave the sanctuary of the borrowed suite.

"I bet Dad hates me because I wasn't the perfect son I was when I was a boy."

"Oh no, don't even think that," Sherry said. "Your dad has been quite concerned about you. He suffered when he didn't hear from you since we left Forest Lake."

"We'll see," Ken said doubtfully.

Five
No Greener Pastures

Ken peered into the kitchen, with Sherry beside him. "Is it all right for us to come in now?"

"You sure can," Mamcu answered.

"After all, it's your house," Tadcu said.

The others streamed into the kitchen. Among them, sixteen-year-old Faith with Kirk, all clean and happy, and Murray, also dressed, clean and smiling.

"Mom and I looked after Murray and Kirk while you and Ken rested," Faith said. Sherry looked gratefully at her mother-in-law then to Faith and smiled. "Thank so very, very much."

"Ken, welcome home, my son," Mother said in Welsh as she hugged him. "It's nice to see you. We hadn't heard from you in so long."

"How are you, Mom?"

Once his mother let him go, Ken hugged his father. "Hello, Dad. How are you?" "I'm fine," Tadcu said, sniffing back tears. "It's good to see you."

"It's good to see you, too, and to be back home." Ken, too, sniffed back tears. "You and Sherry sit at the table," Mamcu invited, "I'll make breakfast."

"I'll hold Kirk for you while you eat breakfast," Faith said to Sherry. "Thank you," Sherry answered.

Murray insisted on sitting on his father's lap. Sherry sat next to Ken as the rest of the children sat around the breakfast table. Mamcu put food on the table and breakfast began.

Half-an-hour later, Ken pushed his empty plate aside and eyed his younger brothers and sisters seated around the table. "My how you've all grown. This community has also put on quite a growth spurt since we left. There's houses, streets, roads and circle drives where there didn't used to be."

"Time doesn't stand still here in Forest Lake like you used to say," his father said. Ken looked at Ricky. "I hardly recognized you. You are a tall, dark-haired man now." "I'm married," Ricky said proudly. He turned to the fair haired woman with violet coloured eyes beside him.

"This is my wife June, and our daughter Gay-Anne."

"Nice to meet you, June."

June pulled back one corner of the blankets Gay-Anne was wrapped in. Ken leaned closer and peered down. "Fair with violet-coloured eyes, just like her mother."

Ken turned his attention to the two younger boys.

"I'm Timmy and I'm thirteen years old," the boy next to Faith said. "And I'm Vincent," the youngest said.

"Timmy, Vincent, if you guys are all done eating, could you go unload the musical instruments?" Ken asked.

"Sure thing." Timmy jumped up from the table and rushed outside. Vincent followed him. Tadcu pushed himself away from the table and turned towards the hallway and the living-room. Ken moved with the rest of the family into the living-room. "Where's Martin?" Ken inquired.

"Martin is married and living in the bottom portion of that house down there," Tadcu answered. "Actually, he owns the building. That's him and Audrey that just came out of the house."

"They don't have any children," Mamcu said. "Who did he marry?" Ken said.

"Audrey Baker."

"Audrey?" Ken said with a shake of his head. "I'm sorry, the name is unfamiliar to me." "She was a friend of mine and Martha's. Her family lives in Lakeview,"

Sherry explained. "Audrey, Martha, Martin and I were in grades nine and ten."

"What about Louise Fraser and Karen Aston?" Ken asked. "Those two girls are from families from the church. I thought Martin would pick a girl more like that."

"He chose Audrey," Tadcu said. "Louise and Karen go way back to the one roomed school house here in Forest Lake. When he started high school, he shared the same seat on the bus to the high school in Lakeview," Tadcu explained. "Audrey was not always a Christian, but Jesus chose to save her."

Ken glanced at his mother. She was smiling. He knew that smile meant that her prayers concerning him, her eldest, the child of her heart, had been answered. He was back home with his wife and family and, best of all, he was back in fellowship with God.

Martin and his family entered the house through the front door. Ken, with Sherry at his side, stood to greet his brother.

He shook hands with Martin, who was surprised at seeing his older brother.

Martin held up his hands for silence. When he had everyone's attention, he said, "I have an announcement to make. Audrey and I have been childless for a long time now. Well, we aren't anymore."

Audrey took one of Martin's hands in hers.

"How many are there?" Ken asked.

"There's five," Martin said without embarrassment. "Quintuplets?" Ken's eyebrows raised in surprise.

"There's a problem," Martin said. "The Children's Aid lady says there's another couple wanting to adopt two."

"You mean, separate them?" Mamcu said, aghast.

"That's right, Mom," Martin said as he reached out and drew Audrey to him and hugged her. "We want to adopt them all together."

"Of course Tadcu said. "We are all behind you and Audrey to help you get the set of five."

Martin turned to Ken. "How long are you here for?"

"I took an extra day arriving here to see about a job in Lakeview. I signed on as Forest Lake's Police Chief Superintendent."

"What?" Mamcu gasped.

"It is rather a commanding post," Ken commented. "I'll be in charge of not only Forest Lake, but the surrounding communities as well. The officer there told me he'd let me know in a couple of weeks about a job."

Ten-year-old Vince suddenly stood up on the couch and looked out the window. "A car has slowed down out on the road."

Faith stood. Sherry reached out to claim Kirk.

Her arms free, Faith joined her brother at the window. "It's coming up here."

When a knock sounded at the front door, Faith and Vincent rushed to the door and returned with a policeman.

"May I speak to Chief Superintendent Kenneth Asquinn?"

"I am Ken Asquinn, sir." Ken offered his hand and the officer shook it.

"You spoke to the Lakeview detachment about job openings yesterday morning." "Yes, sir. That I did."

"Can you start tomorrow?"

"Yes, sir, I sure can," Ken replied. "Wild horses couldn't keep me away, sir." The officer turned and started back to his cruiser.

Sherry walked up to her man and hugged him. "I'm so proud of you, Ken." "Everything's turning out better than I could have hoped for," Ken declared. "But I'll have to apologize to the citizens and try to win back their trust enough for them to want me in charge of the Ontario Provincial Police here in Forest Lake."

"How did you enjoy your time out west?" Ricky asked.

Ken cleared his throat. "I won't say my time out west was wasted. The way God worked in my life is awesome. He brought me from the brink of spiritual, marital, and personal disaster. Even though they were bad years, they show God's victory, and that shouldn't be tossed away." He looked at Sherry and smiled. "I love the name Charlotte but I've come to detest its shorter form, Sherry. It reminds me of the years I spent consuming that useless alcohol and it gave me nothing in return. From now on, I will call you Charlotte and see that everyone else does."

"And we will," Charlotte agreed.

"There's one more thing while we are talking and all gathered here, I may as well keep on with my confessions. I feel really low about causing the accident at Greene's Riding Stable that night. Because of my thoughtlessness and not thinking, a girl isn't walking today."

Adult eyebrows raised around the room. "What's this got to do with you?" Tadcu asked.

"I honked my car horn with the intention of paying that woman back for refusing me a date when I asked her. I thought the horse would buck a little, but I had no idea the crazy animal would do what she did. That incident has caused me many sleepless nights and nightmares."

"Ken, you thought for these past three years that you were responsible for that accident?" Mamcu asked in astonishment.

"Sure. Because I was—am."

"According to the police, it was an accident," Father said. "What?" Ken croaked.

"The truth is, we heard your car horn," Charlotte told her husband. "I thought you had simply honked to say hello, and so I waved back. The horse reared after the half-ton truck passed."

"Huh? A truck?"

"The owner said he'd just speeded up after passing you guys, hit a bump and a fishing tackle box in the back tipped over and spilled all its contents in the truck box. That's the noise that caused Taffy to go crazy and roll on her rider," Charlotte explained.

"You're kidding?" Ken said, looking back and forth between Charlotte, Mamcu, and Tadcu. "Is that true?"

"Yes, it is. I was right there," Charlotte reminded him. "I didn't notice any truck," Ken said.

"You wouldn't. You and Bradan were too drunk to notice anything," Charlotte said.

"I don't know how either one of you could even see to find your way home," Tadcu commented.

Charlotte put her hands on Ken's shoulders and then on his cheeks, and looked into his eyes.

"You are not responsible for Gloria not walking again." Charlotte hugged and kissed him.

Ken sighed in relief of knowing he had not caused the accident. Years of guilt and self-badgering melted away in Charlotte's arms.

"But there is one person in Forest Lake that does hold you and Bradan responsible," Mamcu pointed out.

"Who?"

Mamcu didn't get to answer as a knock sounded at the porch doorway. Murray slid from his Uncle Martin's lap and dashed to see who it was.

"Hi, Grandfather. Hi, Grandmother," he said loudly after opening the door.

"Why, hello, my grandson," Grandfather said while Grandmother smiled lovingly at him.

Grandfather and Grandmother Turehue entered the living room. Grandfather Turehue carried a medium sized cardboard box and Grandmother Turehue some men's shirts folded over one arm. These were set down on arm of the couch. Other church members, Mr. and Mrs. Fraser and Mr. and Mrs. Aston followed, also with boxes of clothes. Some boxes held dinner plates, knives, forks and spoons.

"For you, Ken," Grandfather Turehue said.

"These are some of Bradan's old clothes, but will do until you are able to replace the clothes you left behind," Grandmother Turehue said.

"I hear you are back permanently right here in Forest Lake," Mr. Aston said.

"I will work hard at doing my job as Chief Superintendent , OPP, responsibly," Ken said. "My first job is to apologize to you and others in Forest Lake for my behaviour through my teen years."

"Welcome back," Mr. Fraser said. "I am confident you will handle the demanding responsibility of such a job well. I wish you luck."

"Thank you. Thank you all," Ken said humbly.

"We could use more police patrols in Forest Lake," Grandfather Turehue said. "With the population growth, crime is also on the upswing. And that casino out by the highway causes nightmares for any respectable citizen."

"I'm sure other church members will provide the necessary clothing to replace what you left behind, and, Ken, you and your family are welcome to remain in this house as long as you need," Tadcu said.

"Thank you, Da. I need to thank the church members for being so kind to me and donating the clothing. Me and my family appreciate this."

Grandmother Turehue grasped Ken's arm. "How's my boy?" She asked.

Mamcu folded her hands in front of her. "Oh, if he'd only phone or write."

"Bradan is healthy and doing fine," Ken answered. "We were posted an entire province apart once we graduated the police academy. I was sent to a little town in south-eastern Saskatchewan, and Bradan's on a reserve in northern Saskatchewan."

"Sounds like you have gone through some terrible experiences. Don't ever forget your life story isn't over yet," Tadcu said.

Ken went to the Lakeview police station the next morning. He stood in front of the mayor of Lakeview and the Lakeview Commanding Officer.

"Please place you hand on the Bible here," the mayor said to Ken.

Ken placed his right hand on the leather bound book and raised his left hand.

"I solemnly affirm that I will be loyal to Her Majesty the Queen and to Canada, and that I will uphold the Constitution of Canada and that I, Chief Superintendent Kenneth Murray Asquinn will, to the best of my ability, preserve the peace, prevent offences and discharge my other duties a faithfully, impartially and according to law.

So help me, God."

After being sworn in, Ken left the police station, driving the police cruiser, and turned north towards Forest Lake.

He wasn't patrolling at the moment, but actually looking for a building that could be purchased to use as a detachment office. He'd seen a house for sale across the road from the store/post office and it didn't take long to make that house property of the Ontario Provincial Police in Forest Lake.

In Forest Lake, the April sun had melted all the snow. May went by leaving the yard full of brown patches of grass and trees budding, a promise of a thick, green crop of leaves over the summer. The end of June arrived, the long woodshed at the back of the property was now mostly empty of wood. The one-roomed school house where Martin taught stood empty for summer vacation. The month of June moved into July.

Martin bit off some toast and chewed, as his ears picked up something outside. "Sounds like a car," Martin said.

As one, Audrey and Martin rose from the table and went to the kitchen window to look out.

"It's Mrs. Moore." Martin said. The social worker opened the back door and reached for something inside,

She straightened up and Audrey plainly saw two newborn faces peeking from underneath two blankets.

"She has the babies with her!" Audrey squealed. "Yes," Martin said gleefully.

"Oh, I can't wait to meet those girls," Audrey said. She whirled on her heels and, with Martin right behind, dashed for the door. Audrey had the door open before Mrs. Moore reached the house. She held a bundle snug and warm in fresh blankets in each arm.

"Welcome, Mrs. Moore," Audrey said. "Come in," Martin invited.

Before Mrs. Moore could take a step, Audrey reached out her arms towards the babies, "Please, may I hold one?"

Martin reached for the second newborn. Mrs. Moore gladly handed the girls over to their new parents. She went back to the car and returned with suitcases loaded with goodies for the infants.

"These are the firstborn," she said. "The other three are remaining in the hospital for a while until the doctor is sure they are ready to come home."

Audrey pulled back one corner of the baby blanket and gazed down at her daughter. "What a delightful little girl," she exclaimed. She turned to her husband and looked down at the second baby, "Oh Martin, they are so sweet." Audrey cooed.

"That they are," Martin agreed.

With tears in her eyes and a smile on her face, Mrs. Moore turned and walked back to her car. The first either Martin or Audrey were aware of her having left was when she backed out onto the road.

Inside, Audrey said. "These two look a little alike."

"They are not identical. What shall we name them?" Martin said.

Audrey looked down at the infant she held in her arms, wrapped in a white blanket with pink fringe all around, "This is Olvina."

"You mean Olivia," Martin said.

"No. I mean Olvina," Audrey assured him. "Olvina Audrey Asquinn." Martin looked at the baby in his arms.

"A dark-haired baby wrapped in a mostly grey and white blanket," he remarked. "Look at this." Martin reached out and guided Audrey to the window. Outside in the branches an olive coloured bird, with grey wings and white chest, fluttered around in the branches. The bird was very active and cheerful, always singing its song. *Phe bee, phe bee, phe bee.*

"What is it?" Audrey asked.

"It is a Phoebe, my favourite bird," Martin answered. "I always like their singing."

Phe bee, phe bee, phe bee.

"Phoebe. Let's name her Phoebe Erma, after my mom." "Phoebe Erma is a wonderful choice," Audrey agreed.

"I'm going to take my son and let him experience a cool dip in the wonderful waters of Lake Forest. How about you?" Ken said to Charlotte July evening after the family has finished supper.

Charlotte smiled. "It's sweet of you to invite me."

"Come on, a swim will be fun. It's a hot, sultry July evening," Ken said. He moved closer to Charlotte, expecting to take her hand and help her to her feet, but she turned away.

"I've been on the job two months now, I deserve some relaxation. So do you," Ken said. "I wish I could, but I must hurry and prepare to attend evening classes. My ride will arrive soon."

Ken pulled back and watched in shock as Charlotte rose from the table and went into their bedroom. She came out shortly after carrying some textbooks, pencils and scribblers. A car honked outside.

"Your ride?" Ken asked, and Charlotte nodded.

Ken got up from the table and followed Charlotte outside. At the corner of the house, he watched his wife dash to Martin's car and jump inside. Ken went back inside and to the living-room where the family had moved to.

"How wonderful a cool swim will feel after a hot day of police work," Ken said. "Can I come too?" Vince asked.

Timmy wasn't to be left out. "And me?" "Of course!" Ken said good-naturedly.

"I'll pass this time," Mamcu said. "I'll stay back with Kirk."

After some time in the water with Murray, Ken waded to shore, grabbed his towel and dried Murray, then himself, off. His wet swim trunks did not offer much warmth as the evening cooled. Ricky waited on the dock. Ken walked towards the pier, his son on his shoulder.

Barefooted, Ken easily made the jump from the sandy beach onto the pier. Ken stopped at an overturned canoe . He stooped to allow the boy to slide off his shoulders and onto the wharf.

Ken dried his hair a bit more with his towel.

"I'm really glad you're back."

Ken checked his watch and looked anxiously back at the beach. "Time for Charlotte to arrive home, I would say."

Rick nodded.

Then Ken spotted Charlotte climbing the grade up the ridge to the house, carrying her books. She continued into the house but reappeared shortly. She descended the hill by the railroad crossing and started towards the dock.

Ken met her, and Charlotte kissed him on the cheek. "How did classes go?" Ken asked.

"Excellent," Charlotte said. She turned to Timmy and Vince. "Your Mom says it's time to home and to bed. Time to get you home for bed, Mur."

"Aw, Mommy. Just one more swim?"

"Home. You go with Uncle Timmy and Uncle Vincent."

"Please, Daddy—" Murray began.

"March!"

Murray reluctantly started home with his uncles.

Charlotte said to Murray. "Mommy will be with you shortly. I just want some swim time with Daddy."

"Good-night, Murray," Rick said. "Night, Uncle Rick," Murray replied.

Rick looked from Ken to Charlotte. "Good-night." "Good-night."

"Good-night."

Charlotte looked at Ken who was staring intently at the water. She laughed as she removed her sandals and followed Ken into the water, wanting to swim in spite of her wearing her regular skirt and blouse. The water deepened and Ken dove right in. He surfaced and swam farther away from shore.

"I'm right behind you," Charlotte called and started to dog paddle after him.

They remained in the cool water for a long time, then swam back to shallower water where they splashed and swam about.

"Let's go back to the beach now," Charlotte said, "I'm tired from all this frolicking like a pair of otters in the water. I've had fun, though. I haven't laughed so much in a long time."

"Let's return to the house, then," Ken suggested.

Back at the dock, Ken slipped his jeans on over his bathing outfit,

Charlotte pulled on her sandals and, and with her clothing still damp, the couple started towards the house on the ridge with fingers entwined as they had before they became husband and wife. At the railroad crossing approach they paused before starting up the hill. Charlotte felt as giddy as a new bride.

"Ken, this feels so weird." "What?"

"Me going to this house with you." "Why?"

"Because we've never really walked together to your house together at the end of the day.

Bradan and I always went home to our house when evening came before we were married." "I guess we didn't, but come on," Ken said gently. "It's something you will have to get used to. I know I won't have any trouble getting used to it."

Before either could get very far, a car drew up and stopped and the windows rolled down. "Ken. You again," a voice leered.

"Conrad Cameron and Nigel Weistein," Ken said. "How nice to see you once more." "You come to torment me all over again?" Conrad said.

Evil laughter spilled from the car.

"I thought you and your sidekick, Bradan, were famous policemen out west somewhere," Nigel mocked from the passenger's seat.

"Maybe they got homesick or something?" Conrad said. More chiding laughter came from the car.

"Or something," Ken said. "I'm Chief Superintendent of Forest Lake now." This news surprised the men into silence and raised some eyebrows.

"Really?" Conrad said, nervously. "Sounds like we are really going to have to watch ourselves now, eh, Nigel?"

More wicked laughter came from the two in the car.

"You come and visit our casino," Conrad said. "Maybe you will hit the jackpot and become rich, then you won't have to work as policemen and get nowhere."

Ken felt like shouting, but he kept his voice level as he answered, "Never. You two won't get anywhere living the lives you are. You will both end up in jail, wait and see. I'd rather keep my money and invest it wisely. I love my job. I will be visiting your casino, but it will be to shut it down."

Conrad's lips curled in disdain. "The Gospel Singing Cops." He and

Nigel laughed viciously. "I dare you to try and shut us down." Conrad challenged as he accelerated and the half-brothers sped away in a spray of gravel.

"Ken."

Ken turned at the voice and noticed a figure at one of the screened porch windows. "What is it, Martin?"

"You are wanted on the phone."

"Who is it?"

"He says his name is Bradan," Martin joked. "He sounds anxious to talk to you."

"Okay, tell him to remain on the line. I'll be right there."

Ken tugged Charlotte gently behind as he swiftly climbed the remainder of the hill and entered the house through the front porch doors.

Out of breath, Ken pounced on the receiver, which Martin had rested on the end table. He looked around at those in the room, "May I have some privacy?"

"I will help Murray brush his teeth for bed," Charlotte said and started out of the room. "I'll brush Kirk's teeth," Faith said and followed.

Mamcu jumped to her feet. "I'll help you with the children, too." Tadcu pushed himself up out of the easy chair."I'll see to Timmy and Vince." Martin gathered up his family. "Good time to go home," he said.

Alone in the room, Ken spoke into the receiver. "Hello, Bradan. Good evening to you," he greeted in Welsh, still out of breath from his hike.

"And a good evening to you, too." "How are you?"

"I'm fine," Bradan answered. "And you?"

"I'm fine. You are learning my language just fine. Where are you calling from?" "I'm at our place in Saskatchewan with Martha, Ger and Lyle."

"It's good to hear your voice again," Ken said with a break in his voice.

"The same here. You are all puffed out. Your Mom said you took Sherry and the boys swimming."

"That we did, and we all enjoyed ourselves. And it's not Sherry anymore." "Oh, what do you call her?"

"I insisted we use her beautiful full name, Charlotte," Ken said.

"Then I take it you and my sister have worked out the problems between you. I got your letter. Martha insisted that I call to see if you got home safely and didn't end up in a pile up somewhere."

"We sure have. And more in love than we ever were." "How do you feel now that you've confessed everything?" Ken didn't answer immediately.

"You have confessed everything, haven't you?"

"Oh yes, I've done that," Ken said. "I've confessed everything to God and brought everything out into the open with her and with the family as well."

"So how do you feel now?"

"I feel purged. For once in seven years, I feel clean," Ken said.

"I'm glad," Bradan said. "That's the way I feel, too. I've confessed everything, Martha and I are on a higher love level than ever before."

No one spoke for a while.

"How did we get to be so corrupt?" Ken asked.

"I don't know," Bradan said. "I guess that's just how Satan works. Makes us think another way of living is so much better and then we come to find out it isn't so great after all. I've even given up smoking."

"Me too, and drinking," Ken admitted. "I had an encounter with Conrad and Nigel today.

You remember them, don't you?"

"Oh, I remember the Camerons, alright. Mr. Cameron owned acreage on the choicest spot in Forest Lake."

"That's right," Ken said.

"What did Conrad have to say?"

"Not much." Ken recounted what happened. "Did either of them remember me?"

"Sort of. Conrad asked, somewhat unkindly, where my sidekick was. He had to ask Nigel your name."

Bradan chuckled. "Did Nigel remember? Not that it would break my heart if he didn't. So it is Conrad that owns that wretched casino in Lakeview. I should have known. His father, Arthur Cameron, owned a nightclub in Lakeview when we were kids. The Camerons lived in a pretty nice house, a mansion, from Arthur's profits from that lounge. The Cameron kids always used to tease and torment you Asquinn children because your father couldn't supply you with expensive toys and clothes.

Now they've spread their poison to the poor unsuspecting folk of Forest Lake."

"And that's just for starters. Conrad's casino is not in Lakeview."
"Huh? Where is it then?"

"Right here in Forest Lake at the junction."

Bradan whistled. "Wow. That's bold and a very strategic spot. He'd get business from both north and southbound traffic as well as from the surrounding area. I know they're worried now that they know there's a policeman in Forest Lake. It is not a wide open market for them anymore. When I was a kid, I remarked so many times that the community needed policemen to keep devil worshippers like those two under control. Sometimes it takes getting out of a place to make us realize how much we're needed right where we are, to make us see the value of where we grew up."

"When all the time we were needed here," Ken finished. "Our green pastures were right under our feet."

"I did not find greener pastures here in the west," Bradan replied.

"Well, I've been assigned as Chief Superintendent, which means I'm in charge of the police activities in a lot of communities. You will be glad to know there are openings for more police officers here in Forest Lake."

"Really?" Bradan said in disbelief.

"Yes, really. Come on home with your application and you are hired," Ken said.

"I just received notification from my CO that my time on this reserve is done and I'm to take up a post in the Yukon. Me and my family are all packed up and ready to move immediately."

After a heavy silence, Ken said. "This move to the Yukon does complicate the issue.

What are you going to do, my friend?"

"What can I do but honour my three years in the Yukon Territory," Bradan said hesitantly. "Does this mean the end of a placement for me with you? What about chance for promotions?"

"Not at all and, yes, there'd be opportunities for promotion."

"But nothing like Superintendent or Assistant Superintendent?" Bradan said.

" 'Fraid not," Ken said. "You would be Constable 1st Class."

Bradan feigned a sigh. "Guess I will have to get used to it, Chief

Superintendent. I gotta go now. Give my love to Sherry, er, Charlotte, and tell the rest of the church I miss them all and hope to see everyone in three years."

"And give my love to Martha. Tell her Dad loves her and Mom loves her, and the rest of the family, too."

"I will."

With the click of the receiver, Ken hung up.

Six
Making Peace

Martin awoke suddenly. He shook his head and sat up in bed.

"Huh, what's that noise?" Audrey asked as she did the same. They both listened. The noise came again. "Someone's pounding at the back door," Audrey said. "Who could it be this time of night?"

Martin looked at Audrey who looked back at him. Martin pushed back the covers, grabbed a robe and pulled it on over his shorts.

"We'd better find out. Must be pretty important."

Audrey put on her bathrobe and followed Martin out of the bedroom and across the kitchen. Martin switched on the outside light. A lone woman stood on the step. Audrey quickly unlocked and opened the door when she recognized the lady.

"Mrs. Moore. What brings you here this time of night, or morning?"

"It's five o'clock in the morning," Martin pointed out.

A loud baby squall erupted from bundle in Mrs. Moore's arms.

Audrey was at Mrs. Moore's side in an instant, delight plain on her face. "You've brought another baby."

"The Doctor said today she's healthy enough to be released," Mrs. Moore said. She held out the bundle, which Audrey gratefully accepted. Audrey held her tightly to her and cooed down at her.

Martin turned to Mrs. Moore, "Thank you for bringing her to us."

"I'm sorry to say this, but the next two babies will go to a different set of parents."

The newcomer started to fuss. Audrey held the infant in her arms and hugged her close to her heart. The newborn settled somewhat, but did not stop crying altogether.

"Mrs. Moore, it isn't right for these five babies to be separated...." Audrey began, but Mrs. Moore had already turned and headed back out through the door, another satisfied smile on her face.

Two voices in the nursery started to wail.

"Oh, no. Now Olvina and Phoebe are awake," Martin said.

Audrey shrugged and said to Martin, "We have a new baby to get settled and two sisters to calm down."

In the nursery Audrey, gathered up a soft washcloth, a mild shampoo, and soft towels, then half-filled an infant sized tub with warm water. Martin went to the line of cribs and picked up Olvina and then Phoebe. He joined Audrey. Audrey buttoned up the last of the buttons on the new baby's jumpsuit.

"Wonder what name we can come up for her?" Martin mused. "I like the name Kathleen," Audrey said.

"Kathleen is a pleasant sounding name," Martin agreed. "Our newest baby girl, Kathleen Martha Asquinn."

The parents looked at each other and smiled.

But not one of the three babies was content. Even as Audrey finished the bath and dressed Kathleen in a sleeping jumper, the sisters cried.

Morning broke and there was no peace in the household. No sleep, either.

"I think we should take Kathleen to the doctor and see if she's truly all right," Martin said.

"Olvina and Phoebe are acting strange, too. We should have the doctor check them out again," Audrey said.

"We will drive into Lakeview as soon as the doctor's office is open," Martin said.

"I can't find anything wrong with these three," the doctor told Martin and Martha the next morning.

Back at home, after feeding and cleaning up the three sisters, Audrey handed Kathleen to Martin.

"As good time as any for you and Kathleen to get acquainted," she said. "Oh, I'm beat. I need some sleep."

Carrying Olvina and Phoebe, she walked into the living-room and stretched out on the couch, intending only to rest.

Ten minutes later Kathleen finished her bottle. Martin took it from her and set the emptied bottle on the sink counter. Noticing the silence in the living-room, Martin walked silently into the room. He smiled, and his heart soared with happiness when he saw his wife on the couch, Olvina and Phoebe tucked between each arm and shoulder. All three were fast asleep.

But it was different with the infant Martin carried in his arms. Kathleen started to cry. Martin rocked her and hugged her, "Shussss. We don't want to disturb Mommy."

He quickly returned to the kitchen. "What's the matter?" he asked tenderly. "You three have done nothing but fuss since you arrived. Don't either Olvina or Phoebe like you? Don't you want to be part of this family?"

Martin shook his head. "Daddy's tired. I'm going to follow Mommy's example and get some sleep."

Martin made Kathleen comfortable on the couch alongside her sisters. He fetched some blankets from the closet. He covered Audrey and tucked the blankets around her and the babies.

He then spread a blanket on the floor beside the couch, and using the other one as a cover lay down, and with his head resting on the couch, soon fell asleep.

He didn't know how long he'd slept when the knock on the inside door woke him up.

Audrey and the babies were awake, but Martin had to get up before any of them could. He threw away the covers and hurried to the door. Audrey appeared in the doorway a few seconds behind him, all dishevelled from her sleep. The disturbed babies cried.

"Oh, hi, Ken. We didn't get much sleep last night. The third baby arrived and Olvina and Phoebe hate her. What can I do for you?"

"We're launching the canoe. Care to help participate?"

"I wouldn't miss that for anything in the world. Is there anything we need?" Martin said. He look guiltily at Audrey.

"Go ahead. I'll trail along once the girls are ready."

"We could use a truck to transport the canoe to the wharf," Ken said.

"I know," Martin said. "I'll phone Chester Greene and ask him for the use of his truck." Ken waited while Martin went to the telephone in the living-room.

"He agreed," he said when he rejoined the rest. "What's it all about?" Kirk asked his father.

"Yeah, Daddy, why did you and Uncle Eric and Uncle Martin ask us all to come down here to the docks?" Murray asked. "Why are Grandpa and Grandma Turehue coming along?"

"Settle down quickly and you will find out quicker," Charlotte said.

When all were quiet, Martin signalled to someone by the tracks and Mr. Green's battered old truck started along the pathway to the beach.

"Is that my canoe?" Grandfather Turehue asked.

Ken turned to face his father-in-law. "Mr. Turehue, this is to replace the canoe I was responsible for getting smashed in that storm. Ricky helped build this work of craftsmanship."

When Ken turned to his father. "Dad, I want to apologize to you for being irresponsible enough to lose the tithing money that day."

Mr. Greene backed the car as close to the water as he could, then got out of the car and helped Martin, Eric, and Ken. The ropes securing the craft to the top of the car roof were undone and removed. Ken hoisted the boat over his head and started towards the water. Bradan and Martin followed. Ken lifted the canoe off his head and in an instant the canoe sat in the water.

Once it was in the water, Ken said, "Charlotte, come on. If it pleases you, I will take you and the boys for a ride on beautiful Lake Forest."

"Put on life jackets," Mamcu said.

Tadcu picked out child-sized life jackets from the seats of the canoe. He opened the Velcro-closed front and held the jacket while Murray slipped his arms into arm holes, then he tightened the Velcro strips and zipped up the front. Mamcu did the same with Kirk and the other boys.

"How far are you taking us?" Charlotte asked. "We'll go to the Point and back," Ken said.

Ricky steadied the canoe while the children were loaded.

"Murray, you sit in the front seat," Ken said, then he lifted Murray into the canoe, facing forward.

"Sit really still. Don't move around a lot," Ken told him.

Kirk was helped into the canoe and placed in the middle of the floor.

Charlotte, who held Brian, together with Mamcu and Tadcu watched from shore as the two canoes glided effortlessly through the water away from shore.

Martin watched the canoes from the end of the dock. Suddenly he turned and leaped into a boat moored in a mooring spot, then onto the dock on the other side and started towards the tracks. He had to dodge around several of the young ones before he felt cleared enough to run.

At home, Audrey, along with Faith, and the ever present Bradley Olverton, was ready with with the quintuplets.

"I need to make a very important phone call," Martin said when he arrived home out of breath.

Audrey tried feeding the babies, but each one rejected the bottle. Worry furrowed Audrey, with Faith and the ever present, Bradley Olverton's brow.

"What's so important?"

"Martha. Why didn't I think of her before? We always told each other our woes when we were children. And she's a nurse now."

"So I've heard," Audrey said.

"She ought to know the problem beneath the girls not getting along." He strode into the living-room, sat down in an easy chair, picked up the receiver and dialled the number on the paper.

Martin listened to the phone ring, once, twice then a voice at the other end. "Hi, Martha?"

"Martin," Martha said. "How are you? I haven't talked to you in almost six years. What's up?'

"My family has a problem," Martin blurted out, then plunged in. "my wife and I are adopting children. We have three out a set of five...."

"Like in quintuplets?" Martha asked.

"That's right," Martin said. "But we have run into a bit of a problem. Olvina and Phoebe have rejected Kathleen, the newest one."

"How do you mean rejected?" Martha asked.

"They fuss when the newest baby is around. It started shortly after she was brought here.

The child care lady told us that the next two are going to different parents. The child welfare people aren't letting Audrey and me adopt them all."

"That's too bad," Martha asked. "I don't believe Phoebe or Olvina hate Kathleen or are rejecting her."

"Then what is wrong?" Martin asked.

"You said the child care worker told you, in the presence of the babies, that the remaining two were going to separate homes? They are trying to tell you they want to be together—they have to be together. The five of them are part of a set and they are fighting, in their own way, to be together again. Martin, do you remember the bond between you and me as twins?"

"I sure do," Martin answered. "I was jealous of Bradan when he came into your life. I didn't like him coming between us. It scared me that we were to be separated."

"Then think of Kathleen and her siblings. They are scared to. They need each other, Martin. Don't allow the child care people to leave these five separated another day. They may not live."

"How do I get them to listen?" Martin asked. "Take them to court if you have to," Martha said. "On a teacher's salary?" Martin guffawed.

The bustle of Audrey greeting someone at the outer door drew Martin's attention.

"We have company, Martha, have to hang up now. No wait, it's the child care lady. And there are new crying voices. She must have brought the remaining two. Talk to you later."

"Wait, don't hang up," Martha said. "Leave the phone off the hook. I can hear what's being said. I want to know if the child welfare lady intends to leave the remaining two with you and Audrey."

Martin rested the receiver on the little table and turned to Audrey and their visitor.

"Good evening, Mrs. Moore. A fine evening." "A fine evening it is," the child care worker agreed, "But the couple that wanted to adopt these two don't think so."

Martin and Audrey exchanged glances. "Oh, why not?" Martin asked.

"The husband phoned me this evening to let me know he and his wife wanted me to come immediately and take these two away. They are sick and tired of their crying. They don't want these baby girls. The arrangement is not working out for them."

"I'm sorry to hear that," Audrey said. "What happens to them now?"

"Did you know the phone is off the hook? I thought immediately of you two and how badly you wanted to adopt the five. Are you still interested?"

In a flash, Audrey stepped up to the older woman, arms wide open. "We sure are." Mrs. Moore relinquished the two new infants to Audrey.

"I will hold one," Martin said. Audrey passed one of the blanketed bundles to him. And then a miracle started to happen. The two newcomers continued to cry, but Olvina, then Phoebe, then Kathleen all settled down.

Martin and Audrey continued holding the newcomers, holding each one close to their hearts.

"Why not line them all up together on the couch," Audrey suggested. "That way they will get acquainted and know that they are together."

Martin made sure he was close to the phone's receiver when he said, "Are we doing okay, Martha?"

Martin set the two newcomers down on the soft sandy colored cushion. Gently, Audrey laid Olvina, Phoebe and Kathleen beside them.

"You are doing just fine," a happy voice sang over the telephone. "Their crying doesn't seem quite so distressed. It's more natural now. Good job, both of you."

Martin turned to Mrs. Moore. "The woman that just spoke is my twin sister. She is a registered nurse. I telephoned her for advice concerning the first three, then you showed up. We didn't break the connection."

Suddenly, he stopped talking."Listen."

"All I hear is silence,"Martha said.

"That's right," Audrey said.

"Thanks for your help. Martha.I'm going to hang up now," Martin said.

"What names have you though up for these two?" Martin asked when the family was alone again.

"The infant dressed in the green jumpsuit, I think the name Cassia would suit her," Audrey said. "Cassia Janet, Janet after my mother."

"And it does suit her," agreed Martin. "The baby in the brown jumpsuit, I pick the names Eunice Marjorie."

"Marjorie sounds oldish, but a fresh and lovely name," Audrey responded. "And she's named after an aunt in Wales," Martin said.

The young parents, arms around each other, stood gazing down at the five babies snuggled together on the couch cushions, Olvina with her arms around Kathleen.

The next morning at work, Ken drove along Highway 11 towards Forest Lake. He crossed over the little wooden bridge spanning the river flowing south. He slowed as he approached the casino at the junction.

He didn't bother going in, this time, but he did stop and survey the entrance of the casino.

After a few minutes, a group of pre-teens marched boldly across the parking lot and into the building. They were obviously not concerned about any police presence. They knew there was no reason to fear the police in this place—until now.

Ken decided to walk through Forest Lake and talk to some of the citizens to get their take on the crime scene. He drove through portions of the town that hadn't even existed when he was a kid. Where there had once been just rock ridges and brush there were now bustling communities.

Ken noticed the railroad maintenance section car parked on the siding which ran through part of the town. Five section crew workers were busy pounding pins to hold a section of rail in place. Ken walked up to the foreman who appeared to be in his sixties. Grey hairs peeked out from under the brim of his black-and-white striped railroad cap.

"Good afternoon, Gus Olverton," he said and shook hands with the man. "I'm the new OPP officer for Forest Lake."

Mr. Olverton turned to the working crew, and said, "Listen to this."

Four railroad crew workers put down their hammers and picks and gathered around their foreman and Ken.

One looked at Ken turned and said, astonished, "What? A policeman in Forest Lake?" "It's nice to have a law officer patrolling our roads and back roads," another said.

"Too much drinking and mischief goes on at those isolated spots after dark," was another opinion.

"Chief Superintendent. But you're so young," Mr. Olverton

said. "How old are you, twenty-one? How many years' experience as a policeman?"

"I'm twenty-six," answered Ken. "I have nearly four years' experience. I know that isn't a lot, but I don't see another policeman applying to be transferred here. I grew up here and want to serve the citizens of Forest Lake and surrounding area."

Three younger members of the crew harrumphed at this.

"Well, nice to know some of our young people are starting to take Forest Lake seriously," the middle-aged man said kindly. "I'm behind you."

"So am I," said the foreman.

Ken shook hands with the five men and resumed his walk.

Next, he came upon a group of citizens seated on the steps of the store. Some were seated on chairs on the deck in front of the store while others were seated on the steps, the store owner among them. Ken walked up to them and greeted the group after enduring a moment of shocked silence from those on the step and the platform at seeing a policeman in front of them.

"Good morning, everyone. I'd like to hear what your main concerns are in this community," Ken said.

When no one answered, Ken looked at the store owner, "Winston, we will start with you."

"Shut down the casino," Mr. Turehue said.

"It's drawing our children away from attending church on Sundays and causing them to play hooky," a man seated on a step right in front of Ken shouted.

"It's causing those that can't afford to gamble to go there anyway and play the money needed for food and clothing and other expenses away," a lady, Ken presumed to be the man's wife, said.

"A lot of teens that were doing good in school have quit and are spending what money they do get at the night club," another added.

"I have that casino under surveillance day and night," Ken said.

After this initial outburst, the group fell silent. The teens in the group shot Ken hostile looks, but generally he received smiles of welcome from the adults.

"Sir, are you the Chief Superintendent for the whole area?" asked a senior-aged man in the back.

Ken turned to face the group again.

"Yes, Mr. Newton, I am. Newly sworn in."

"We're behind you," Mr. Newton said.

"Good luck in your job," a lady said. She stood and shook his hand. "Thank you, Mrs. Weston," Ken said.

With the citizens' statements of support ringing in his ears, Ken took this as an indication that he should leave.

"Thank you very much for your input," he said and turned and started towards the police station to finish up his paperwork before heading home.

It was a mild mid-January. Ken drove out to the river beyond the last of the houses on the east side of Forest Lake. He turned the cruiser around at the rickety railroad-tie bridge and started back.

He came to what had been Greene's Riding Stable. The corral, hitching rail area was chocked with snowbanks three feet deep. The riding horses were no more although the barn still stood. Two pairs of workhorses grazed on hay from a bale set before them in the snow.

Suddenly, an idea flashed through Ken's mind. He turned into the driveway leading to the house and parked by the side porch.

He dodged puddles of melting snow as he walked up to the door and knocked. To his surprise, it was opened almost immediately.

"Afternoon, Mr. Greene."

Mr. Greene looked Ken over closely.

"What do you want? I haven't seen you since the canoe launching. Martin asked to use my truck. You are one of those drunken bums that spooked my horse and caused her to roll on her rider."

"No, I'm not," Ken said hurt at Mr. Greene's words. "And Chester, please stop saying that I am. You know and I know it isn't true.

"I had to get rid of that beautiful horse and shut down my trail riding business because of you and your friend. She was much too intelligent an animal for most riders to handle. It took an experienced horseman or woman to ride her," Mr. Greene ranted on.

"I realize that, now. I'm sorry about the accident, sir. But, neither I nor my friend was responsible."

"Get out of here," Mr. Greene shouted. "I didn't want you on my property then and I don't now."

Ken tried another approach.

"I'm asking people what they think is the most important crime to deal with in this town. What do you think, Mr. Greene?"

Mr. Greene answered in the same tone.

"Drunken driving should be stopped. There's too many teens ripping up the roads and doing all kinds of damage on the weekends. Arrest them."

"A good idea," Ken agreed.

For the first time, Mr. Greene really looked at Ken and took notice of the uniform he wore. He rubbed his chin. "Well, well, you didn't desert Ontario after all. You really are Forest Lake's child."

"Yes, I am, and always will be. But more importantly, I am a child of God."

"You wear the uniform of the Ontario Provincial Police well," Chester Greene said. "Thank you," Ken said, humbled. He didn't know why it felt so good to hear Mr. Greene

say that. He touched the rim of his cap then turned and walked back to his car. As he drew closer to the vehicle, he heard a voice call urgently over the radio.

"Chief Superintendent Asquinn, please answer immediately. Urgent!"

Ken sprinted the short distance to the car and reached through the open window for the radio receiver. He pressed the button and spoke into the receiver. "Chief Superintendent Asquinn speaking. What's so urgent?'"

"Your wife was taken to the hospital by ambulance twenty minutes ago, sir," the voice explained.

"Is she in labour?" Ken asked. "Yes, sir."

"I'm on my way."

SEVEN
CASINO SURVEILLANCE

It was the first day of February, three weeks after the birth of Brian. Outside, snowflakes fell gently to the ground. Ken was about to walk out the door for his Wednesday day shift.

Murray and Kirk were seated at the table. Charlotte stood by the sink, Brian in her arms.

"Dad has stood and firmly preached the entire counsel of God throughout his ministry at Golden Ridge Baptist Church. I intend to attend the service this evening after work and we will attend from now on as a family.

"Yes, Ken," Charlotte said.

A sudden thought struck Ken. "I am going to get into the habit of saying a prayer even before I start my work day and I'm starting right now."

He said to Murray and Kirk, "You two, please join us."

The boys jumped up from their chairs and moved over to where the others stood. Ken joined hands with his family. He grasped Brian's little hand in one of his and Murray's hand in the other, and the family bowed their heads.

"Father in Heaven,

"Thank you for this wonderful day and for the blessings bestowed upon this family. I now ask for strength and wisdom to face my day at work. May your guardian angels watch over each of us while I am away.

"Amen."

"And please be with Bradan, Martha, Gerry and Lyle," Charlotte inserted.

"I must be off now," Ken said and went out the door. "I'll be home for supper and the mid-week service this evening. If I don't end up working overtime."

Ken did not have much time to be unoccupied that morning. It seemed that the mischief makers were just as busy mid-week as on the weekend. They'd been at it all day and had just gone to bed and another bunch had taken over for day hours. A lot of vandalism, and one house had been broken into.

He patrolled the walkways and streets, some he knew well, and others were not familiar at all. After his drive around, he parked his cruiser in front of the police station and started in the direction of the public beach.

Here he came upon a party goer that had not been able to find his way home and was sleeping it off under a tree.

Ken helped him to his feet and retraced his steps back to the station, the man leaning on him for support.

"No use leaving you out there to sleep on the hard ground and end up with frostbite," he said as he lowered the fella onto a cell bunk bed. "I will be back in a while and let you out of here. By then you should be awake."

After locking the cell, Ken changed into plain street clothes. He replaced his policeman's hat with a fisherman's headgear, then drove out to the highway in his personal car..

Ken got out of his car strolled towards the casino entrance. As he walked across the icy parking lot towards the entrance, he observed that the gambling house did a brisk business. There must have been fifty cars parked on the grounds.

A heavy-built guard looked at Ken as he approached, and Ken nodded at him as he pushed opened the door and stepped into the foyer. He removed his heavy down-filled parka and hung it on a hanger along with the other patron's coats. No words passed between them.

There were a lot of kids at the slot machines lining the hallway. Ken recognized a local boy. Kirby Weston was only sixteen but he missed more school classes than he attended. With a lot of time on his hands, he was beginning to be troublesome around Forest Lake and communities beyond. Terry Weston, while alive, had been Conrad's lieutenant in witchcraft, was his grandfather. Kirby's father, also named Kirby, had been the only survivor of two sons, in a house fire. Terry had died. The fire had been intended to get rid of Ken, but backfired and Terry died instead. There were lots of reasons for the Westons to hate Christians.

Ken opened another door and stepped inside past the second guard. Immediately, talking and laughter, the *clickety-clack* of slot machines, and the stench of cigarette smoke greeted him. At the bottom of the stairs leading up to the offices were situated, a heavy glass door. Next to this door was another, thick and made of wood. As Ken surveyed, three men knocked on the door and after repeating something, it was opened quickly to them then closed.

Must be Conrad's office. Through floor-to-ceiling windows, he saw a party of men and women and a boy no more than two enter the room. He recognized Nigel and realized he didn't recall ever seeing Conrad enter the building or the office. A withered, grey haired man sat at a table in one corner of the office who was likely a clerk.

He'd need more time to get familiar with Conrad's activities.

Right now, his mission was to find office, so he started up the stairs. When he did find the office, he found someone there, but it wasn't Conrad just lots and lots of girls standing about.

His eyes took in a crystal chandelier hanging from the ceiling above the gambling table while a three-bladed fan hung from the ceiling above the table by some easy chairs in the middle of the room. A clock hung on the wall above the door. A small couch and three easy chairs sat to his left with round, wooden coffee tables between them.

At the feet of one of the woman, Ken noticed a child on the floor with a picture book open across his lap. Ken figured the woman to be the boy's mother and perhaps Conrad's son. Two bottles of wine stood on the table.

Behind the couch was a piano and floor-to-ceiling bookcases and more pictures. Scarlet velvet drapes hung open from curtain rods.

Through an open door at the very back, Ken could see bedroom furnishings. He could only imagine what went on here.

Does the little boy sleep here while drunkenness and gambling goes on all around him? Ken wondered. *Not a good environment for a child to be raised in.*

"What are you doing here?" A man approached him menacingly from the end of the hall. "I'm sorry. I must have taken a wrong turn. I was looking for the bathrooms," Ken answered.

"They are downstairs," Nigel answered in a tone that told Ken he was expected to leave immediately. Ken hurried backed out the door and hurried down the stairs.

When Ken returned to the station, he glanced at the clock on the wall above his desk. He sighed, reached for the telephone receiver and dialed..

"Hello, Charlotte," he said when the telephone was answered at the other end. "Look, darling, I'm running a bit late. It's already 6:45. Church starts at 7 0'clock. I plan to attend the service, but might be a bit late. A drunk has been in the cell long enough. I should be able to release him now."

Ken listened, then said. "Thanks for be understanding, dear. I'll be with you and the boys shortly."

Ken hung up, stood up and returned to the cell area.

After seeing the sobered-up drunk out the door, Ken again glanced at the time. Almost seven o'clock. He changed out of his disguise to his regular street clothes, locked up the station and drove home in the cruiser. He had worked an eleven hour day. By now supper would be over and church goers preparing to attend the service.

Ken parked the cruiser in front of the house. On the driveway between the house and church he saw Charlotte with Brian in her arms, Kirk holding onto her hand, and Murray skipping a few steps ahead, walking towards the church. Martin and Audrey walked beside them, Audrey pushing a six-passenger baby stroller.

Murray turned to his mother, "I'm right, Mommy. Daddy won't be in church tonight.

Daddy's a liar."

"Liar," Kirk echoed

Charlotte said sharply, "Your Daddy will join us when he can." Ken lengthened his stride and soon caught up with the group.

Ken hugged his wife and kissed the top of her head, then Murray and Kirk. He placed a kiss on Brian's forehead.

Charlotte shot Murray a meaningful look. Murray hung his head in shame. "Sorry, Daddy," he said.

"Me too," Kirk wasn't to be left out. Ken was taken aback at the apology. "Sorry for what?"

"For calling you a liar," Murray said. "I called you that because I didn't think you would join us for church this evening."

Ken knelt and wrapped his arms around both boys. "I love you both. But, there are lots of little things that can make Daddy late. I had to work a little longer than I wanted to."

Charlotte kissed him. "Glad you made it in time."

Ken peeked at the two new babies. "So the child care people allowed you to adopt all five?"

"Yes, they did." Audrey's smile told it all. "May I hold one?"

With Martin and Audrey's permission, he lifted one and then the other. "And their names are?" Ken asked.

"The infant you're holding is Eunice," Martin said. "Beautiful, like her sisters," Ken said.

"And the baby you returned to the stroller is Cassia," Audrey said. Ken returned Eunice to the seat in the stroller.

More people arrived. More men, women and children alike gathered to admire the two new infants

"You two are doing an awesome job with these five girls," Charlotte complimented Martin and Audrey.

"Thank you, Ma'am," Audrey said.

"I will carry Brian," Ken said to Charlotte. Ken and his family moved up the church steps.

"Good evening," Mr. Aston, Charlotte said to the man sweeping snow off the steps. "Good evening, Ma'am, Ken," Mr. Aston returned the greeting.

Ken saw Grandmother and Grandfather Turehue arrive at their pew. He smiled at them and they smiled back. It would soon be time for Pastor Asquinn to come out of his office, get

behind the altar and start the service. Pews began to fill up. Ken left the back of the church. Charlotte, with Murray and Kirk followed Ken, with Brian in his arms, to the family pew near the front. Other members of the Asquinn family started filling up seats around him.

Ken looked Charlotte's way, tears trickled down her cheeks. He brushed them away tenderly. Charlotte smiled him. "I'm glad work didn't keep you away."

"I'm so glad you are here, Daddy," Murray said. "Me, too," Kirk said.

Tadcu appeared. "Welcome to the mid-week service." "Let us start with hymn 624 in our hymnals," the song leader said.

Whenever a hymn was sung or the congregation stood for any other reason, Ken always held Brian in one arm. Murray and Kirk stood close to Charlotte's knees.

Ken had never felt so happy in many years. He sneaked a glance his mother's way and saw her smile back at him.

The next Sunday morning, after the last hymn and before he started the sermon, Pastor Asquinn said, "We are in for a treat this morning. Ken has agreed to share his testimony with the church. Ken, if you would come up to the front."

Ken handed Brian over to Charlotte, and made his way up onto the platform. From behind the pulpit, Ken looked down over the congregation. The church was a lot fuller than usual. More townsfolk, as well as those from outlying communities, had decided to attend church today. Mr. Greene beamed happily back at him from the rear pew.

Ken cleared his throat and the congregation turned their attention to the front.

"I really don't know where to begin. This is because it isn't clear to me where my backsliding began. It must have been back in grade nine when I entered high school. Satan subtly threw temptations my way. He deceived me into believing winning in sports was the only way to go and that losing was a disgrace. He made me believe attending after-school activities, such as football games and Air Force Cadets were more important than mid-week church. During these events, I usually stayed with a classmate in Lakeview. It got so that I stayed away from home and church more and more.

"Usually, after winning a football game, or cadets, we'd put on a party with lots of drinking. Satan deceived me into believing that I enjoyed myself, and that I could enjoy myself in sin all I wished because, after all, I was a believer and regularly attending a Bible-believing church. He threw in the sin of pride, along with the temptations of riches and fame.

"At the age of ten or around there somewhere, maybe even eight years old, my dream was to become a policeman and join the Ontario Provincial Police and fight the bad guys right here in Forest Lake. As I grew older, this police force and the hamlet of Forest Lake seemed too tame for me. I wanted greater adventure and a job that could offer me wealth to enjoy a good life for me and my family. I began to get lofty ideas and switched to training for the RCMP.

"Oh, that well-known police force brought me recognition and I was well onto my way to owning material wealth. But was I happy? No. Why? I did not include God in my plans. I did not ask him whether he wanted me with the RCMP. These thoughts were really the desires I clung dearly to. I allowed Satan to enter my life and control it. He drew me away from the church and prevented me from learning about the way I should be going. I wanted worldly gain. I wanted to be famous. I wanted money. I wanted position. I thought I had outgrown God. Well, I got all these, or at least I was well on my way to reaching my visions, and almost lost everything I owned and loved in the process. My wife left me and returned to Forest Lake with our two sons with the intention of divorcing me.

"Those that called themselves friends told me to forget about Charlotte, to find another woman to take her place and move on, after all, isn't that what most successful men do? Most of them go through several wives. Charlotte asked me for a divorce, and I was about to grant her what she wanted, but God intervened. That was one letter he did not permit me to send.

"I didn't want to divorce. I'd learned about true love by observing my parents while growing up and through the teachings of this church. I realized I would lose my wife if I didn't go after her. Her worth to me is beyond earthly measure. I praise God that Charlotte has forgiven me."

Ken paused as he tried to reign in his emotions. He pulled a handkerchief from his pocket and dabbed at his eyes.

"I don't care to recount where I have been, but I know where I am now and where I'm going. I'm on my way to my heavenly inheritance, guided in this life by the Holy Spirit. Jesus has reached out his hand for me to grasp and keeps me going in the way I should go. He restored to me the joy of his salvation and restored my home. With His help, my family and I will continue to walk in God's way.

"There is one lesson I learned from my frolic and it's found in Titus 2: 14 – 'Who gave Himself for us, that he might redeem us from all iniquity, and purify unto himself, a peculiar people, zealous of good works.'

"It is clear to me what he saved me from. He saved me from a life of slavery to sin, and now works within me to purify me and make me into a vessel for him.

"Along with getting in harmony with God's will in my life, I have greater rapport with my wife and sweet fellowship with my sons, Murray the firstborn, then Kirk and the baby, Brian.

"No more chasing after dreams merely to feed my pride and for the friendship and praise of the flesh. My walk will be with God and I will seek His guidance every day."

Ken dabbed at the corners of his eyes.

"Once I thought I had to rule my household with a heavy hand. Now I ask God to give me wisdom to be a partner to my spouse with mixed consideration and gentleness. Charlotte, my lovely sunbeam, I love you and I'm sorry for all the heartache, pain, and loneliness I caused you. You are my life. There is no earthly measurement that could gauge what you are to me.

"And I don't want to leave the rest of the community out. I want to thank the citizens of Forest Lake. Most have reached out and embraced me, and supported the work I have to do here. And Dad, I'm sorry for the way I treated the Lord's money that afternoon you gave me a simple task to carry out."

Ken was through. Before he could step off the platform Charlotte, baby in one arm, and Murray and Kirk following, walked up to him and hugged him with her free arm.

Tadcu stepped behind the podium. It was several seconds before he could get his emotions under control.

"Thank you, Ken. There is a definite humility about you that was not present before. Now that you are humbled, He seems to be lifting you up."

"Thank you, Dad," Ken said. "In order for God to work out His plan in my life He had to allow what happened to happen. I chased after elusive dreams and transparent rainbows and looked for greener pastures thousands of miles away from home and this assembly while all the while he wanted me right here in Forest Lake."

There were "Amens" from the Pastor and congregation.

"I truly believe the praying wife that loved you through it all is the very core of this tale."

Tadcu looked around at the congregation, "For those that call this your home church, I ask for a vote on whether Ken should be reinstated as a member of this fellowship. "Who's in favour?"

"Aye," voices shouted.

"And those against it, say no," the pastor said.

There were a few scattered "nos" from the members.

"Ken, you are now a member of good standing in this church. Now the sermon."

When the sermon was over, Ken and his family made their way to the back of the church.

Men and women, shook his hands, congratulating him and welcoming him back to the church fellowship. Mr. Greene stopped by the family group.

"I don't know what all this means about what just happened to you, but I must tell you, you have lived a very interesting life."

Ken waited in his cruiser, hidden by tall grass at the junction. From this vantage point, he could keep an eye on the casino as well as the school bus stop. This called for him to be up and on duty much earlier than his usual hours, but he did not mind and his wait was rewarded.

Once the bus stopped to load children waiting to board, some teenagers slipped off and sped as fast as they could towards the casino. Some of the students that should have been boarding decided to follow them. Shortly after that, a plain black car slowed and turned into the parking lot, then drove right up to the entrance way and stopped. The driver got out and opened the back door. A man, woman, and little boy stepped out onto the gravel. The man wore a disguise, and he was too far away for Ken to be able to recognize him. The little boy started to cry and his mother, Ken guessed, hit him hard on the behind. The boy jumped around and screamed in pain.

"That poor child," Ken muttered. "This looks like a case for the child welfare people."

Ken picked up the pair of binoculars from the seat beside him held them to his eyes and focused. Almost instantly the man came into focus. The man wore a wig of greying hair almost down to his shoulders, leaned on a cane, and pretended to be stooped and frail. But there was something about the man's features that made Ken's spine crawl. When the man turned his head, Ken was able to get a better look. Ken remembered those features that seemed to be set in stone from their days in the Forest Lake School. One of the women said something he didn't like and immediately Ken noticed a change in him. For one thing, when angered, his eyes shot fire and his face took on a devilish look.

"Conrad. He's been right in front of my eyes all along."

Ken started the cruiser's engine and drove the short distance to the nightclub and parked, intending to follow Conrad and his party to Conrad's office.

When Ken arrived outside the door to Conrad's office, the door was closed and padlocked. A note taped to the door said:

"Closed until Wednesday of next week. Management."

"Oh no," Ken groaned, "Conrad and his friends weren't arriving, they were leaving."

A year later, in late October, a snow storm blanketed the area. Ken parked his cruiser in the casino parking lot, opened the door and stepped out into ankle deep snow. Snow from an early storm beat against him, and the wind buffeted him. He grasped the car for support for a moment or two before starting across the parking lot towards the casino entrance.

He paused by other cruisers waiting and waved his hand, indicating for them to follow.

Ken and his help overpowered the lone guard at the front door. Ken nodded, indicating for them to proceed him inside. An officer broke the glass enclosing a fire axe and used the axe to smash glass door by the stairs to the upper level. The group of officers headed up the stairs, and down the hall to the Conrad's office door. Here the policemen stopped, and Ken signalled for one of the officers to knock.

"We are the police," the officer said when a muffled "Who's there?" came through the door. "Can we come in?"

"No, you can't," a male voice answered.

Ken nodded at his backup, and one officer kicked in the door. The door opened into a twenty-foot by forty-foot room. Ken looked around. Although others were in the room, only one person sat at a small gambling table although five purple cushioned chairs stood around it. The man was the old bent-over gentlemen. A pile of poker chips and a wine bottle, along with an overflowing ashtray and a regular telephone sat in the middle of the table.

Ken turned to the man who pretended to be old and lame. "We have a search warrant." "So?" the old man sneered.

"I want to see this warrant," Nigel said.

Ken showed his distant cousin the required paper. Nigel barely glanced at it.

Ken looked at the questionable ladies. He noticed one looked heavy with child. "Where is your boss?"

He received only raised eyebrows and silence. They would have spit on him if he'd been closer.

"Seize those," Ken ordered, and the officers with him began to grab witchcraft masks from the wall and one seized a cape hanging on a rack by the back door.

Ken said, "Nigel Weistein you are under arrest."

Out of the corner of one eye, Ken saw Conrad's dark features twisted in that aggravating sneer.

"I'm—we're not doing anything illegal," Nigel stammered. "They want to gamble, so we're here to fulfil that desire."

"You mean you want to fuel that desire," Ken corrected. "We are arresting you two and closing this place down. You and Conrad are operating on an expired licence, and for earning in excess, every evening, the amount of money allowed by the gaming laws. You two bring in $3000 while only $1000 is allowed. You and Conrad are being fined for encouraging youth of Forest Lake and area, under the age of eighteen to gamble."

Nigel waved a hand. "You can't be serious. You can't arrest Conrad. He is not here." Ken smiled. "He's here."

Ken watched the old man's eyes turn red, his features more like the devil than anything human.

Ken moved closer, his pistol still trained on the two gamblers, to handcuff them, his backup right behind him. He instructed one to handcuff Nigel, while he turned to the second male.

"You, Conrad Cameron, are under arrest."

Ken was about to handcuff Conrad, but before he could do the job Nigel threw a bundle of loose papers at him. Hundreds of pages floated through the air, obstructing the policemen's view, and the two half-brothers dashed for the door. They were through it in an instant and fleeing along the corridor, down the stairs and towards the entrance.

"Go after them," Ken instructed two of the men who charged after them. From the window of Conrad's office Ken could see that Conrad and Nigel were already downstairs and running across the front lounge to the doors. Police officers sprinted down the stairs and out to the parking lot. By the time they reached the parking lot, Conrad and Nigel were in Conrad's car and speeding out to the highway. The policemen ran to their cruisers and were soon in pursuit.

Conrad and Nigel had quite a lead.

Ken spoke into the mike of his radio phone. "Lakeview, I need backup immediately. A tan-coloured, four-door Chevrolet Malibu, licence plate XOE-OHO with two suspects inside is headed south. My guess is the licence number is fake and they will try to hide out in Lakeview."

"10-4. On the way," answered the dispatcher.

Crying coming from the room at the back of the office caught Ken's attention. He exchanged questioning glances with his helper. Ken strode towards the room, his companion following. He held his fingers to his lips, signalling for his helper to not make a sound, then to open the door. The Constable pushed gently on the door, which opened only a crack. Ken and the Constable stood silent, listening. Ken pushed the door wide open and the young toddler he'd seen before in the office lay in his crib, amongst filthy and soaking wet blankets, crying. Ken and the Constable exchanged horrified looks.

The thin figure cowered against the bed, back up against the lower frame. He put a hand over his face when he heard someone else was in the room.

"No, no," he cried.

Ken and the Constable looked at each other in disbelief. Ken took a step towards the boy, but the youngster jumped over to the other side of the bed.

"Leave me alone!"

Ken walked slowly to the end of the bed and proceeded extra cautiously towards the boy. "We aren't here to hurt you."

The boy continued to press up against the corner, not trusting. Ken crouched and talked to the youngster in a comforting voice. He held his hands out to the boy who cowered away from him.

"Come to me," Ken said softly. "Please."

Ken spied a candy bar lying on a chair. He reached out and picked it up, tore off the cellophane of the top half and broke off a tiny chunk. He held it out to the child.

"Come to me and we will see that you get some clean clothes. Would you like that? And something to eat?"

The boy looked at Ken suspiciously for several seconds, then slowly walked towards him. Ken drew him into his arms and wrapped his arms around him. The boy struggled for a while, then settled down and rested his head on Ken's shoulder in acceptance.

"What's your name?"

But the youngster only sniffed and chewed at the chunk of candy bar.

When the boy continued to chew and didn't answer, Ken turned to his companion. "Find out if Conrad Cameron has a son."

Ken stood up, his charge still in his arms, "I don't see your parents around. I know just the place to leave you and you will feel right at home. Come downstairs with Constable Parker and me and we will meet a nice lady. Is that okay with you?"

The boy nodded. Ken took some tissues from a Kleenex box and wiped the boy's eyes and nose, then started towards the door and the stairs to the lower part.

"All is terrifyingly quiet," Ken said to the officer who greeted him. "Have arrests been made and the prisoners transported out?"

"Yes, sir," answered the constable. "And the patrons?" Ken asked.

"They were ushered out and told this place is closed down permanently. A 'closed by police order sign' hangs on the doorknob."

"Good job," Ken said.

Ken's companion returned. He handed Ken some papers, which Ken read through thoroughly.

"There's a woman waiting to see you, sir."

He turned to an elderly lady standing to one side. "She says she's from the child welfare.

Mrs. Moore, meet Chief Superintendent Asquinn."

Mrs. Moore stepped forward, arms outstretched. "And this is the child you want me to take into custody?"

"Yes, Ma'am," Ken answered.

"And I have just the place for you to go to," Mrs. Moore spoke kindly. "There's children there just your age. Sound okay to you?"

"Want to go with Mrs. Moore?" Ken said softly to the boy. The boy nodded.

Ken set his burden on the floor. Mrs. Moore reached out and offered her his hand. The child clasped the bigger hand in his.

Ken told the lady as she turned to return to her car. "His parents abandoned him in this place. Can you imagine that?"

Mrs. Moore rolled her eyes. "A child in a casino."

Ken turned to speak to the officers. "I will meet you at the Forest Lake station. I have a matter to take care of."

In his car, Ken spoke into the radio mike, "Have the two suspects from the casino been captured yet?"

"Yes, sir, they have."

"I want a full report when I arrive," Ken said.

Just minutes later, Ken pulled up behind Mrs. Moore's car where she parked it in Martin and Audrey's driveway. It was early morning and grey streaked the eastern sky.

Ken accompanied Mrs. Moore and the boy to door and knocked. It opened almost immediately and Audrey, Kathleen at her side, stood in the open doorway.

"Ken! Mrs. Moore! It's a couple of years since we've seen you, Mrs. Moore. How are you?" She stared wide eyed down at the boy. "And who's this?"

"Martin," Audrey called back into the interior of the house. Her husband, holding Eunice's little hand in one hand and Olvina's in the other. Phoebe and Cassia appeared in the hallway shortly after. He looked at Ken and the welfare lady, then his eyes fell on the child. His eyes opened in wonderment.

"Another charge?"

"He's a relative," Ken said.

"A relative?" Martin said, then his eyes grew wide in disbelief. "You're kidding? You aren't talking about Conrad's son, are you?"

"Actually no," Ken replied, then dropped a bombshell. "He's Nigel's son. But he might be expecting a sister or a brother, or a cousin. I noticed at least one woman in the group at the casino is pregnant."

After a moment's debate, Martin looked at Audrey. "If he needs a home, bring him in," Audrey said.

Olvina took the newcomer by the hand.

"Come along," Audrey said to the girls and gently led the way into the kitchen.

As Ken turned to leave, Martin looked at him and said. "I don't know about this one, Ken. Nigel's son."

"You are free to name him whatever you want," Mrs. Moore told Martin. "The name won't make the difference," Martin said.

EIGHT
FOREST LAKE'S SONS

Charlotte walked into the living room and stood in front of where Ken sat with Murray and Kirk on either side of him. Murray held Brian on his lap. Ken held a story book open on his lap, reading to the children. Charlotte kissed Ken's head.

"Thanks, darling, for watching the boys this evening."

Ken kissed Charlotte back. "You are welcome. You can call on me anytime you need a babysitter, as long as I'm not working."

"Daddy, it's Saturday and you have started your days off," Kirk said.

"And I don't have to hurry away to night classes," Charlotte said. "Darling, you have to work long hours before the luxury of days off."

"That's because Daddy's the only policeman in town," Murray said. Ken set the book aside. Charlotte lifted Brian from Murray's lap. "Murray, Kirk, Brian, bedtime."

Ken stood up. "I'm taking my family to Turehues' General Store for ice cream." Murray and Kirk cheered and Brian kicked his legs as he caught on to his big brothers' mood.

"But it's bedtime for the children," Charlotte protested. "So, we will ignore their bedtime this one time," Ken said. "But...." Audrey started to protest.

Ken put an arm around Charlotte's waist and pulled her to him. "Come on. It'll be fun."

Charlotte still didn't seem convinced so Ken kissed her on the forehead.

"Okay," Charlotte agreed at last. "The children get to stay up past their bedtime, but only this once."

"Certainly, only this once," Ken agreed with a little smile. Ken dragged out the baby carriage and set Brian inside. "Are we walking, daddy?" Murray said.

"Yes, we are. It's such a beautiful evening and I feel the walk will do us all good."

As the family started out for the store, the breeze whispered in the trees and the birds sang sweetly. Once again the months and seasons marched on; cold winter suns turned to strong summer sun rays. These rays melted away the snow that blanketed the land and ice that filled the lakes and rivers. Waves pounded the lakeshore beyond the tracks.

"It is a beautiful evening," Charlotte said as they walked.

Murray was content to remain close to his mother and father and younger brothers. He skipped along next to the carriage his mother was pushing, talking to Brian. Ken carried Kirk on his shoulder.

When they arrived at the store, Charlotte lifted Brian out of the carriage so Ken could set it on the front platform where it would wait while they went inside. Ken spied the older man watching their approach through the large front window by the check out. Mr. Turehue hurried around to the door, and held it open. Charlotte ushered Murray through first, then Kirk. She followed, carrying the baby, and Ken entered last.

"Good evening, Grandpa," Murray greeted. "Good e'ning," Kirk echoed.

Brian just squealed and laughed.

"Good evening to you all in return," Mr. Turehue said. "What can I do for you all?"

"Daddy's buying us all ice cream cones," Murray blurted out. "All except Brian, he's too young."

Grandfather Turehue looked at Ken who smiled and nodded, then hurried over to the ice cream cooler. "Well then, ice cream it is. What shall I dish out? Murray, what's your favourite flavour?"

"I like any flavour as long as it's ice cream," Murray said. Everyone laughed.

"Tell Grandfather your most favourite flavour," Ken said. "Go on. This is the evening we all order what we like best."

"I want rainbow flavour," Murray answered. "Me, too," Kirk said.

"Two rainbow flavored ice cream cones coming up," Grandfather Turehue said pleasantly. He topped a cone with ice cream and handed it to Murray.

"There you are, my grandson." "Thank you, Grandfather Turehue."

He topped another and handed it to Kirk. "T'ank u," Kirk said politely.

"Plain old vanilla for me please,Dad," charlotte said.

"And the same for me,"Ken said.

Soon all four licked away at their ice cream cones. "Have you heard from Bradan lately?" Charlotte said.

"He phones now and again. He and Martha are both eager to get back here to Forest Lake. Bradan's simply waiting for his three years in the Yukon to expire and he will be on his way. He has six months to go."

"That's right," Ken said.

Grandfather Turehue looked concerned. "With all this changing places of residence, even provinces, first he left Ontario to train in Saskatchewan, and now he wants come back to Forest Lake. Where will the money come from?"

"Bradan told me he still has most of the trust fund you started for him when Dad bought the house from you."

Grandfather Turehue breathed a sigh of relief. "I'm glad to hear that. It shows he was not totally irresponsible over the past few years. It's time for me to close up for the night," Grandfather Turehue said as they finished their cones. "If you don't mind waiting an extra few seconds, Ken, could I walk with you?"

"That would be nice, Dad," Charlotte agreed. "We'll just get Brian settled in the pram." The group walked on. They arrived at the entrance to what used to be the Camerons'

estate. Ken suddenly stopped and took Charlotte's hand. Charlotte looked at him, surprised. "Come with me, my darling. I have something I want to show you and the boys. Mr. Turehue, you are welcome to accompany us, if you care to." "I sure will."

"Let me," Ken said and Charlotte stepped away from the stroller so he could push Brian.

Ken still held her hand while Murray clasped her other hand and Kirk clung to his brother's hand. Grandpa Turehue wrapped his fingers around Kirk's tiny fist. Ken led Charlotte up the driveway to the Cameron house.

"Ken, where are you taking me?"

Ken continued along the driveway. "I'll tell you in a minute."

At last they stopped on the front step where Charlotte admired the splendor of the house and accompanying grounds.

"What beautiful grounds and a splendid house," she said. "The surroundings could be amazing. Look."

She pointed towards a hedge where a man in coveralls, work boots and a peeked cap, trimmed the hedge. Hearing the sound of a lawn mower, she looked and saw a second man on a riding mower, mowing the lawn. She gasped in amazement at the lady who held a long-handled cleaning mop and washed the upstairs windows until they glistened in the sun.

Charlotte's eyebrows knit in puzzlement. "Why are the Camerons so intent of the upkeep of the house and grounds all of a sudden? Are Conrad and Nigel moving back? Makes me wonder what the inside of the house is like. I'm glad I don't have to find out. What are we doing here, darling? Aren't we trespassing?"

"Not at all, Charlotte, my dearest. This is our new home." "Ours?"

"Ours."

Charlotte withdrew her hand from Murray's grasp threw her arms around Ken and hugged him tightly. "Since when?"

"Since Nigel and Conrad were arrested. Neither of them will be needing the place anymore. See, I have the key."

He turned the knob and the door swung open.

"We will view the interior now, my dear," Charlotte said.

Ken lifted Brian out of the stroller. Charlotte took Murray's hand in hers and Kirk's hand in the other and stepped inside ahead of her husband.

"I will look around outside," Grandfather Turehue said.

Ken followed Charlotte and the boys inside and shut the door.

Charlotte was rendered speechless the instant she set foot inside. The house was spic and span. In the upper part of the house, a woman dressed in older clothes and a rag wrapped around her hair, polished the railing to a gleam.

"This is the first time I've been in this house," Charlotte said.

"I know."

"Have you ever been in here before?"

"Nope. Well...that's not quite right. Once, long ago when Conrad and Nigel held Martin prisoner in their house for several hours."

"How soon can we live in it?"

"As soon as we can get moved in, and I would like that to be before I go back to work."

Ken and Eric positioned the last chair, in the living-room.

"Now to hurry and get everybody ready for Charlotte's graduation this evening," Ken said to his younger brother.

Ken sat up straight and proud in the auditorium of the community college in Lakeview, with Brian seated next to him, then Kirk, and Murray last. Mamcu and Tadcu sat beside Murray.

Ken turned his head so he could see the back of the room. Soon music started and the graduating class started down the aisle and up to the platform.

Ken and his family waited while several names were called. His heart swelled with pride when the Master of Ceremonies said, "Mrs. Charlotte Julia Turehue Asquinn."

Charlotte stepped forward. Ken and his group clapped loudly as Charlotte walked straight and proud up to the MC. He handed her the square piece of paper that changed her life completely.

The ceremony over, Charlotte hurried to the table where her party sat and fell into Ken's arms.

In the Yukon Territory, Martha and Bradan arrived home from working the day shift. The two boys met her at the door. She took off her nurse's cape and hung it on a hanger.

"Mommy, can I stay with Daddy?" Gerald said.

Martha smiled. "Why sure. Daddy can use some help putting the Jeep away for the night."

"Me too," Lyle said.

Martha nodded her consent, and the two boys scampered off to join their father by the garage.

Martha entered the house and joined the babysitter in the entranceway. She, too, was in a hurry to start home. Bradan and the boys entered rather noisily. The housekeeper tried to get through the door on her way out as Bradan, Gerald and Lyle tried to get in.

The phone rang.

Bradan scrambled to answer it. "Hello." "Who is it, Daddy? "Lyle asked excitedly.

"Who's calling?" Gerald jumped up and down in his eagerness to know. Bradan lowered the receiver, "Say hi to Uncle Ken and Aunt Charlotte."

"Hi, Uncle Ken, Aunt Charlotte," the boys spoke into the receiver and squealed with delight when they heard their aunt and uncle's voice.

"Hi, Gerald. Hi, Lyle."

"This is the first call from you in a long time, my friend."

Martha said, "They had just finished moving into their own place since we heard from them last."

She moved closer so she, Gerald and Lyle could listen in on the conversation.

"The Yukon Territory is both cold and beautiful," Bradan said and Martha heard Charlotte chuckle.

"The summer's are nice," Martha said.

"It's fine. What's up with you?" Bradan said.

"We have another son," Ken said. "We named him Brian. He's twenty four months old."

"Is that so? Martha is pregnant. The baby will be born six months from now. We're praying for a daughter. We've picked out the name Shannon. In case you haven't heard, Martha is also a registered nurse now."

"I know. Charlotte is through studying." Ken said excitedly. "She graduated this evening. We no sooner returned home from the ceremonies and we just had to phone and let you hear the great news. She will teach from grades one to four in the new Christian school."

Charlotte hastened to explain, "The one-roomed school we attended is talking about shutting down."

"Why?" Martha said.

"Attendance has dropped enough to make it too costly to keep the school operating. The congregation at the church are looking into buying the building and using it for a Christian school," Ken said. "Additions will be built on as required."

"Charlotte, I'm glad for you," Bradan said. "Ken, any ideas what you will do with your property out west?"

"I've already sold the house and grounds. Now, I have no ties at all to my time there." "Perhaps now is the right time for me to use the money in the trust fund to buy a place in

Forest Lake," Bradan mused.

"And start all over again," Ken said.

After a pause Bradan said, "How weird, talking about starting all over again in Forest Lake. I was born and raised there."

"Me too, almost," Ken said. "We are Forest Lake's sons."

Six months later, when the days started to noticeably lengthen in March, Bradan listened to the telephone ringing at the other end. Martha stood close to him to hear the conversation. The four old friends kept in touch this way a lot. Someone answered on the first ring.

"Hello."

"Hello, Ken, my friend."

"Hello, Bradan. It's good to hear your voice again."

"How is everything there in good old Forest Lake?" Bradan asked. "Gwd ."

"Ken, Charlotte, I delivered a daughter this time," Martha said, elated. "Her name is Shannon."

"Congratulations," Charlotte said.

"I'm happy for you," Ken said. "Bradan, mai da dyn, there is now an opening for more officers in this department. Are you still interested?"

"Interested? I sure am."

"Bradan only has a year to go on his term," Martha said.

"It's time to start thinking about a house close to Forest lake," Bradan said. "Are there any on the market?"

"There's a cottage across the alleyway from my house. Did I mention we are now living in the shack that used to belong to Arthur Cameron?"

"No, you didn't. Shack? I don't remember that place as a shack."

"Yes, we would be interested in the house across the alleyway from you," Martha said. "I don't recall a house or an alleyway behind the Cameron house," Bradan said.

Charlotte chuckled. "There is now."

Ken said, "There's a lot you don't know about Forest Lake. The main road we once knew starts right by the corner entering Forest Lake and around Golden Ridge to the corner close to your place and west again to join up with the road out to the highway. We, at this end, can take care of obtaining the house for you and your family. How do you like that idea?"

"I like the idea," Martha said.

"So do I, although we will be buying the place unseen," Bradan said. "Wow. I can't wait to get back there.

Bradan felt something weighing down his feet. He looked down and saw Gerald clinging to him. He quickly said to Ken.

"Ken, I must hang up now. Ger is vying for my attention." "Okay. Talk to you later, my friend," Ken said.

"I'm glad you are home, Daddy," four-and-a-half year old Gerry said when his father hung up.

Martha walked to Bradan's chair and sat down on an arm. She hugged her husband and son. "Yes, dear, we do like it when you are home at night."

Gerald, then Lyle yawned.

"Time for bed," Martha said. "We need our rest. We have church tomorrow." "That we do," Bradan agreed.

The next morning Martha waited in the living-room with Gerald and Lyle. All were dressed in their church clothes and waiting for Bradan to join them.

"Where will we go to church, Daddy?" Gerald asked

"We will continue to attend church at home," Bradan declared. Lyle seemed stricken with the idea. "I like church at home?" "Daddy will teach us," Martha said.

Bradan pulled a chair away from the kitchen table. "We will all be seated."

Martha helped the boys into their chairs, then she gathered Bibles and hymn books and handed them out. Bradan reached for his guitar.

"We will start our worship service by turning to hymn 42," Bradan said.

Martha helped Lyle, then Gerald to find the page. Bradan strummed on the guitar, then started to sing. Martha, Gerald and Lyle joined in happily.

"That was God-honouring singing," Bradan said when they had finished the first hymn. "One more, then I will get into the lesson."

The second hymn sung, Bradan set aside his guitar. He pulled his Bible closer to him in preparation to teach. The boys and Martha opened their Bibles and listened intently as their father taught them the scriptures.

Martha listened to the phone ringing at the other end. It was a whole year since she'd last held a telephone conversation with her friend Charlotte. She couldn't wait to give her the news.

"Nos dan, Charlotte," she said the minute the phone was answered. "Da iwan," Charlotte responded.

"This house is sold and we're ready to move," Martha said. "The furniture movers are already on their way. Bradan's busy loading our personal belongings in the station wagon. We plan to get a good night's sleep tonight and start out as early as we can tomorrow morning."

"We will put the furniture in place in your house. All you and your family have to do when you arrive is start living in the house," Charlotte said.

"We appreciate that," Martha said. "Good night to you too, my friend. Llawer o gariad to you and yours."

"Good-night, Martha, Bradan," Charlotte said.

Martha hung up and immediately turned to Bradan. He and the boys had just come in from loading. He pulled Martha into his arms.

"We've finished packing up our children and belongings and returning to Ontario," he whooped. He was as elated as a child opening gifts on his birthday; so was Martha.

"Come on, Ger, bedtime for you and Lyle," Martha said when they'd all settled down.

At four o'clock the next morning, Bradan said to Martha, "Load the children in the jeep."

With the baby, Shannon, in her arms, Martha did just that. "Ger, Lyle, get in the car; Daddy says we are ready to leave."

Gerry skipped and leaped his way to his daddy's maroon and white 1968 Plymouth Fury Station Wagon parked in the driveway, already packed with luggage and other belongings, and the back seat chock full of Bradan's musical instruments.

Bradan left the house last, the real estate agent who had been entrusted with the task of selling the house right behind him. Bradan made sure all the doors and windows were locked and otherwise secure. He handed the key over to the agent, then walked towards his waiting family. He took one last look back at the house and the SOLD sign in one corner of the yard, shook hands with the agent and climbed behind the wheel.

"Is it far to Forest Lake, Daddy?" Gerald wanted to know. "It sure is. It's where I was born. It's in Ontario."

"Will we be living where Uncle Ken and Aunt Sherry live?" Lyle said. "We sure will be," Martha said.

"And you will see your cousins Murray and Kirk," Bradan reassured his son. "Oh boy!" Gerry was thrilled.

"And Brian," Martha added, "and Olvina, Phoebe, Eunice, Cassia, Kathleen, and Malcolm."

"Who are they?' Gerald asked.

"They are your new cousins," Martha explained.

Bradan shifted the gear into drive. "Forest Lake, here we come."

Martha smiled at him. "Your face glows with even more anticipation than when you said practically the same thing as when we came west."

Even though Forest Lake had experienced changes while he had been away, Bradan had no trouble finding the house when, five days later, he and his family arrived back in Forest Lake.

"Here's the place!" He signalled and turned into the driveway. Welcome homers stood at the bottom of the steps as Bradan pulled in and parked. He remained behind the wheel, gawking at the surroundings as his family poured out of the car.

Martin, Tadcu and Mamcu rushed towards them as Grandfather and Grandmother Turehue welcomed their only son with open arms. "Welcome home, son."

Mamcu hugged her daughter. "Welcome home, Martha."

"Thank you, Mother," Martha said through tears of joy. Martha handed Shannon over to her mother and turned to her father, and then her father-in-law.

"Welcome home, Martha," said Grandfather Turehue.

"Thank you, father-in-law." Martha spoke in Welsh without thinking. "Whoops, there I go again."

Martha then turned to her twin and the two embraced.

"Welcome back," Martin said. He held out his hand to Bradan and the two shook. He turned to the woman standing beside him. "This is my wife, Audrey."

Martha squealed as she and her old friend, Audrey, hugged. "I'm so glad you married my twin brother. I never thought, back in high school, that this would happen."

Martha noticed two toddlers standing in front of Martin.

"Meet Olvina and Phoebe," Audrey said, gazing down at the two toddlers. "And this is Cassia, Eunice and Kathleen," Martin said.

Bradan joined them and looked with delightful surprise at Martin and Audrey's family.

"Who is this?"

"Meet Sihon," Audrey said. "A boy we are fostering."

Martin whispered to Bradan, "Sihon is the name we gave him. His real title is Grant Weistien."

Bradan looked at Martin startled, "Weistien? As in Nigel Weistien??"

Martin nodded. "He's a good boy. He even loves going to church. He has since the first Sunday he lived with us."

Martha held out her arms, "May I hold them?"

Each quintuplet was lifted and hugged, then Sihon. "Where are we, Daddy?" Gerry asked.

Grandfather Turehue smiled down at the boys. "And which one of my grandsons are you?"

"I'm Gerry. And this is Lyle."

Grandfather Turehue had brought a couple of sweets with him. He handed the gummy chewy candy to Gerald.

"Thank you," Gerald said, wide-eyed.

Martha and Bradan smiled as Gerald politely handed one to his brother, before popping the other in his mouth. The boys smacked their lips in great enjoyment.

"Thank you, Gran'father," Lyle said.

Grandmother Turehue looked towards the baby in Mrs. Asquinn's arms. "And that is Shannon, Gran'ma," Lyle said

Ken and the children joined the group. Ken hugged his sister. "Welcome back," he said to Martha.

Martha smiled at a small boy clinging to his Daddy's pant leg. "And this must be Brian?"

"That's right," Charlotte said. "He's two-and-a-half." "Good, now we can look at the house," Martha said.

Martin stood beside Martha with Bradan on her right side as the new arrivals looked around. Bradan's vision shifted to the house.

"Not a big house," Bradan said. "Built more to the standards of Forest Lake in the 1950s."

The house stood on a cement foundation with a large addition at the back. Wooden steps led up to a deck and to the porch. On the deck sat a swinging seat with a canopy over top, along with other deck furniture. There was a screen door on the outside and a solid wood door as an inside door, but a window filled one wall between the door frame and the corner, another window on the middle of the south wall.

Inside the porch, Bradan and Martha noticed another window. Long, tall, curtained windows on east side were open to allow the breeze to flow freely through. In the front, cement steps with a wrought iron railing and peeked roof led to a screened front door. Inside, the inner door was open to allow the breeze from the lake to blow through. A large bay window took up one south wall to the left of the door, while to the right another tall, slim window probably belonged to a bedroom. Above, was a loft also with windows open.

"But the house, Ken," Bradan said. "You called it a mansion. The house is smaller than the one we lived in out west."

Martha gazed around at what was her home. "Bradan, I love this house. It's quaint and blends right in with Forest Lake. Lots of room for a flower garden. Did the movers arrive with our furniture yet?"

"It's all in place inside," Mother said.

"Vincent, Timmy, move the stuff loaded in my car into the house, please. I may even pay you," Bradan said to the two eager young men.

Martha said, "Well, come on, let's go inside."

"Here are the house keys," Grandfather Turehue said and handed Bradan the key chain. Bradan turned to the rest. "You all may as well come in, too."

With Martha at his side, Bradan went up the stairs. He unlocked the porch door, then opened the screen door and the inside door. The porch was well equipped with coat hooks for winter clothes and space to leave winter boots, caps and mittens. At the very back were two doors, both open. Martha paused to peek through the doorways. They were bedrooms, boys' bedrooms. There was an immediate turn to reach the door into the house. This Bradan unlocked then stepped aside to allow Martha to enter first.

Martha stepped from a sun-filled porch into an equally sun-filled kitchen. Facing west was a tall window partway open with a screen. A gentle breeze helped freshen the room. Lining most of the east wall were cupboards and the sink, with a small window

Martha stopped by the sink, rested her two hands on the edge and looked out the small window. From here she could see the green and white one roomed school house. She turned and looked at Bradan who had come up behind her. He put his arms around her.

"It's been done. This school we all attended together has been shut down and the public school children bused into schools in Lakeview."

"A Christian school is replacing the old system," Martha said.

"Gerald and Murray will be the very first two to start learning in the new school," Bradan said.

With memories lingering, Martha and Bradan turned away.

Bradan walked to the refrigerator and opened the door. It was filled with food and pitchers of ice cold water, and milk for the children.. Martha moved to the door at one end of the kitchen and discovered this to be the bathroom. The usual here – sink, bathtub, medicine chest, towel storage, vanity and a flush toilet.

On the left was another bedroom. Martha peeked inside to discover the room was set up for girls.

From there, Martha and Bradan moved into the living room. There was a front door and on its right another long, slim window and another doorway which Martha walked towards, Bradan beside her. Inside was the master bedroom.

She had walked past a staircase leading to the upper part of the house.

"What's up there?" Bradan asked.

She and Bradan climbed the steps and peeked over the railing.

"A nice sized loft," Martha said. "This room will be my sewing room."

"And there's lots of storage space," Bradan said, looking at empty rooms.

Next, the couple went back downstairs and out to the porch and turned to the door leading to the basement. Most of the basement was open, but there was a laundry area with washer and dryer ready to go.

Before they went back upstairs, Bradan opened the freezer and lifted out some steak, and other packages of meat. Upstairs, he and Martha went outside where the guests waited. Bradan, Martha at his side, paused on the deck. He beamed his bubbly smile down at them. Martha also smiled.

"I want to thank all that had a part in setting everything in order so all we have to do is move in," Martha said.

"I will start up the barbeque and we'll enjoy a meal outside on the lawn," Bradan said. "There will be steaks, salads, mashed potatoes, hamburgers as well as hotdogs and marshmallows for the little ones."

"What better way to have a house warming party?" Martha said.
"The weather is perfect," Bradan added.

Everyone stayed.

Once the food was ready, but before anyone could take the first bite, Bradan gathered everyone around to say the blessing.

He bowed his head, and the group followed.

"Thank you, Father in Heaven, for our safe return over those many miles of treacherous highways to be back here among friends, family and church members. We now ask you to bless this food we are about to delight in. Please bless all the hands that helped prepare it. Amen."

Bradan picked up some barbeque tools to start barbecuing. His father tied an apron around his waist and stood beside his son.

He picked up some barbequing tongs, held them up for Bradan to see and said, "I'm ready to help."

Steaks were sizzling on the grill when Bradan glanced towards the road and noticed a couple coming towards him. One rode in an electric wheelchair.

Bradan turned to his father, "Dad, can you look after the barbeque? There's a couple of people I want to talk to."

"Sure, son."

Bradan set down his tools, whipped off his apron and started down the driveway. Ken edged his way through a crowd of youngsters and joined his friend.

When he and Ken stopped in front of the couple, Bradan said. "I know you two. Jim and Gloria."

"That's right," answered the girl in the wheelchair.

Bradan turned to the man and shook his hand. Bradan turned to Ken. "You remember my buddy, Ken?"

"Oh, yes," Jim said. "Yes," Gloria answered.

Ken shook hands with the two newcomers. "Are you married to Jim?"

"Yes," Gloria answered hastily. "No," Jim said.

Gloria's face turned red. "We aren't married, just living together. Not marrying has nothing to do with my disability. We wanted to go with the trend of living-together instead of marriage."

"We heard you were back, Bradan," Jim said. "We just stopped by long enough to welcome you into the law enforcement job here in Forest Lake. You, too, Ken."

"I've thought about you two, especially you, Gloria, a lot over the years and wondered if you've had a good life," Ken said.

"We've had good years," Jim said.

"Gloria, I'm terribly sorry about that night." Bradan looked the wheelchair over, meaningfully.

"What night?" Gloria asked.

"The night that horse crippled you," Bradan said.

Gloria touched Bradan's hand. "I'd like to forget about it and move on."

"Me too," Bradan agreed. "Say, why don't you two stay for the barbeque with us?" Bradan offered.

Gloria was about to say no, but Bradan stopped her by holding up a hand. "I won't take no for an answer, and besides, it'll be fun."

Two more plates were brought out, more steaks added to the grill.

With the last steak taken from the barbeque, and plates filled as full as they could get, Bradan settled into a bench chair on the deck. Martha sat beside him. From her position she could see their two boys playing with Murray and Kirk. Built in between the two chairs was a small table for food and drink. Bradan set his plate on the table and started to eat. A few feet away, Ken and Charlotte on the swing chair pushed gently back and forth with their feet. Brian, who was in Charlotte's arms, liked this and laughed and giggled.

Mamcu brought tall glasses and a pitcher of iced tea outside where the friends sat in lawn chairs. She poured a glass for Bradan and set it before him, then refilled glasses for Martha, Ken and Charlotte. She'd brought Styrofoam cups along with her and she filled cups for the children and passed them out.

"I feel, for the first time in ten long years, that I'm doing God's will." Bradan said.

"Me, too," Ken said. "For once in a long while, I know where I am, and where I'm going, and how to get there. The Holy Spirit leads me now. It makes me out-and-out ashamed of myself the way I wanted to get away from Forest Lake, the church, my upbringing, Dad, and go off searching for greener pastures in faraway places."

"Amen to that," Bradan said. "There were no greener pastures; not where I was, anyway." "Me neither," Ken said.

"When I was a boy, I often commented on how Forest Lake needed policemen to keep certain kinds of people in line," Bradan said. "As I grew older it seemed that this hamlet had nothing to offer. After being away and coming back, my eyes have been opened and I can see where I was needed all along and the greener pastures are right here under my feet."

Bradan sipped his iced tea.

"I hear you my friend," Ken said, as he sipped his.

Bradan set his emptied plate on the little table.

"That was a wonderful meal. I'm so full and lazy I couldn't get into any kind of mischief."

"I wouldn't even if I wanted to," Ken replied.

Bradan sat back in his chair with his feet resting on the railing. Martin leaned against the deck railing not far away. The rest of the guests were seated all around. Murray and Gerald now sat on their respective father's knees. Audrey and Faith were pushing the quintuplets and the younger children in some swings in the children's playground in one corner of the yard.

"Which way did you travel?" Ken said.

"The TransCanada Highway, Northern route. At the junction into Forest Lake, I stopped to fill up and to give the family the chance to stretch their legs. I had a chance survey the buildings."

"Highway Gas Station was once the casino Conrad ran along with his half-brother, Nigel," Ken said.

"The casino you closed?" "Yes, it is," Martin said.

After a pause, Bradan suddenly sat up. His feet landed noisily on the wooden deck floor and he snapped his fingers.

"I know!"

"This must be good," Ken said with anticipation.

"And there's our guitars leaning against the wall," Bradan said. "What a stellar plan." Ken's eyes shone with excitement.

"We'll sing from right here where we are," Bradan said to Ken. "There's lots of room here."

Martin sat beside his twin and Charlotte and listened as Ken and Bradan strummed their guitars and sang.

At the end of one song, Bradan sighed and said, "It's so nice to sing spiritual hymns again."

"Having the burdens and uncleanness washed away certainly feels good," Ken agreed.

They sang a few more songs and then Bradan said, "That's all for this evening."

Ken and Bradan slid the leather straps from their shoulders and set the instruments aside.

Bradan led the way upstairs.

"We could form a two-man band and call ourselves—let me see..." Bradan paused and thought. "What was that name Nigel called us?"

"The Gospel Singing Cops," Ken supplied the name.

"That's it!" Bradan said. "We will be known as the Gospel Singing Cops." "Conrad wasn't complimenting when he called us that," Ken pointed out.

"I know," Bradan said. "But we'll make it work. Wait and see. We can meet and practice here whenever we feel up to it."

"We can arrange something like that," Ken said, then added with a broad smile. "And maybe it'll save on the girls' nerves and ear drums."

Martha kissed Bradan. "I don't mind at all."

Charlotte hugged Ken. "We are both glad to have the two of you home." Ken yawned, though he tried to hide it behind one hand.

"Must get some sleep. I've had a busy day today and expect another one tomorrow." "Me too," Bradan said and feigned weariness just to tease his buddy.

"I will see you tomorrow morning at the police station at eight o'clock, sharp," Ken told his friend, then added jesting. "That's in the morning,"

"Yes, Chief Superintendent," Bradan jested with a mock salute.

Ken rounded up his family and headed for home. After that, the other guests quickly dispersed.

Bradan stretched and yawned. "Finally, we're alone..." his words trailed off when he saw Martin and his family were still in the room. "Oh."

Bradan looked towards the outside door and nodded, indicating he wished Martin to follow. Bradan walked behind Martin to the door and stepped outside onto the step and followed him to the ground.

"Is there something on your mind?" Bradan demanded.

Martin couldn't look his brother-in-law in the eyes. Martha and Audrey stepped out onto the top step and remained there, waiting.

"I'm really glad you are back," Martin began. "I know I didn't show much heart about you marrying my twin sister right from the time you said you loved her and planned to marry her. I was jealous."

"Why?"

Martin pushed his hands guiltily into his jeans pockets. "I felt, as my twin, there was a bond no one else had the right to come between."

"You felt that Martha should remain unmarried all her life in order not to violate this bond between you?" Bradan said. "I realize twins do have a bond, but would you want your sister to go unmarried because of it?

Martin hung his head further. "Remember, I was only ten years old." Martin suddenly looked straight at Bradan. "But now that I'm married to Audrey and have her to love and lean on, I realize how you feel about Martha, and how she loves you. I wouldn't want her married to anyone else. I would not want anyone to come between the relationship between Audrey and me."

"Thank you," Bradan said. "Does that make us friends?" Martin nodded. "Yes."

"Good," Bradan said. He turned and included Audrey in his words. "Now, please excuse me, I must get some rest."

Bradan sat in the front seat of Ken's car. Ken sat behind the steering wheel while Martin sat alone in the back. Ken had parked alongside the road to watch a string of trail riders move across an open field running parallel to the road.

"Now!" Ken shouted and leaned on the horn.

Horrified, the boys in the car watched as Taffy screamed, rose on her hind feet, flayed her front hooves in the air in front of her before going over backwards and rolling on her rider.

"Floor it, Ken! Let's get the hell out of here," Bradan shouted.

Bradan startled awake, the sound of Ken's car speeding away full in his ears. Martha and the children were already up. Bradan dressed and walked into the kitchen.

"No wonder I'm tired. It's only three o'clock in the Yukon. My system has not gotten used to the time change yet."

But Bradan's words didn't fool Martha.

"You had another nightmare about Gloria and Taffy?"

"I thought coming back home would end the nightmares," Bradan said. "Will they ever stop?" Martha said.

Nine
Patrolling the Byways of Home

Martha kissed Bradan before he went out the door, smiling. The walk to the police station took only ten minutes. He found the doors already opened and Ken at his desk when he entered.

"Bore da," Ken greeted him.

"Good morning," Bradan returned the greeting. He couldn't resist teasing his friend with a rebellious yawn and quipped. "I'm to report to a Chief Superintendent. Can you direct me to him?"

"I think I can do that," Ken bantered back.

Bradan chuckled, but soon let out an out and out laugh. The moment his mirth bubbled forth, so did Ken's and the two of them had a good laugh.

When they'd recovered, Ken looked at some papers on the desk in front of him. "I uncovered your application. This is it here."

"You mean you haven't reviewed it?" Bradan said, astonished.

Ken looked at Bradan and joked. "Why would I have to review your application? How long have we known each other, my friend?"

"I feel like we have been friends all our lives," Bradan said.

"That's how I feel," Ken said. "So why do I need an application to help me decide whether or not there's a position here for you?"

Ken fell silent, and Bradan waited for him to say more. "Is there a position here for me?" "Of course there is."

"And when do I start?"

"You started the instant you walked through that door, if that's okay with you." "It certainly is okay with me. I love the idea of patrolling the streets of home."

"Then, Constable First Class Turehue, you and I are partners. I will see your promotion goes through immediately. Let's just not let rank get in the way of our friendship."

"Okay."

"Welcome aboard, Bradan. Welcome to the Forest Lake Detachment." The two friends shook hands.

"I look upon you as a man of Christian integrity personified," Ken said. "There's not another man on the face of this planet I would rather work with."

"There's no one but you'd I'd rather work with," Bradan said.

"You wear the OPP uniform well." Bradan complimented his friend. Ken leaned over and reached for something beneath the desk. "There's one more thing."

"What's that?" Bradan asked, not sure whether he should be nervous or not.

Ken came up with a Bible in his hand. "You must be sworn in as a peace officer." "You can't imagine how great I feel at this moment," Bradan said.

During the Sunday evening service Ken and Bradan were scheduled to sing together. From behind the altar, Bradan looked across the congregation until he brought his gaze to the front and looked down at Martha where she sat with the boys and Shannon. Martha smiled encouragingly back at him.

Bradan and Ken stood before microphones, waiting expectantly.

Bradan said, "I realize most have heard me and Ken sing before, and know how strong my faith and testimony had once been. To tell you the truth, I'm a bit nervous now, wondering if the elders would consider my belief to be as strong now, or stronger? It's good to be back up here. We've been away from singing far too long."

He and Ken strummed a few notes to tune and a thrill ran through

Bradan. What a delight to hear such sweet music from the guitar once again. Bradan glanced around at his singing partner, smiled at him, and could tell by the smile Ken returned, that the singing and music stirred his emotions, too.

The two started singing. Bradan and Ken held their heads high, keeping eye contact with the congregation. Joy filled Bradan's heart to see families once again seated quietly in their family pews watching them. The song ended. Bradan led the way across the platform, down the three steps and to their seats.

Bradan wiped moisture from his eyes as he sat down beside Martha and Ken took his seat next to Charlotte, Murray, Kirk and Brian.

"Bradan, did you have a testimony for this evening?" Tadcu asked. "That song was testimony enough, but is there more you have to share?"

"Yes, sir, I do."

Bradan returned to the altar. "Thank you, Pastor Asquinn." To those seated he said, "I've been a dunce."

This brought a ripple of laughter throughout the congregation.

"No, seriously. I have been a half-wit. For ten long years, I willingly followed Satan's cunning ways that fooled me into thinking I was having a good time. He led me into bars where he deceived me into thinking I couldn't live a proper life without all that they had to offer. I drank until sometimes all my reasoning and senses were gone and, yes, at times I experimented with drugs." He had to pause in his speech and gather his emotions under control before continuing. "I can only thank God I did not get hooked on any of those senseless drugs. I cheated on my lovely and long-suffering wife. I took God's name in vain."

His voice broke and tears glinted in the corners of his eyes. "Can you imagine that? I took God's holy name in vain. And, for what? Simply for the approval of the flesh, position and money. But, through it all, my tolerant wife stayed with me. She prayed for me. Martha, my precious one, when you get to heaven that's when you will fully understand how profitable these prayers were.

"I know now my dreams were lofty, but fame and fortune came to nothing. Like Brother Ken, I was well on my way to owning a fancy house and position in the community, but I did not once stop to seek God's approval of my plans, or seek out whether what I wanted was actually His plans. By this time, all that other stuff, including money and position, seemed like nothing and had lost its appeal and splendor. I can tell you now that God has steered me in the direction I should go.

"I feel a lot more blessed and richer now that I'm walking again in harmony with God and His will. I have great rapport with my wife and sweeter relationships with my sons and now a daughter. This is what truly makes a man rich in this life. I will close this testimony with Isaiah 38:15 - 'I will go softly all my years in the bitterness of my soul', meaning I will walk humbly and meekly all the rest of my days on earth, remembering what the Lord saved me from."

"Amen," said Martin and Da. "Yeah, I hear you," Ken said.

Bradan had to struggle with his emotions for several seconds, but, before he started to speak again, had them under control.

"Martha, I am sorry for all the heartache and loneliness I caused you. I know I don't deserve such a partner as you, but I thank God continuously for giving me a Christian wife. I know when we married, I bought you a very expensive wedding ring and fooled myself into thinking I did my duty towards you. How wrong I was. I've since learned that rings are merely a symbol, only God can unite and make a couple."

There were "Amens" from the men.

"I have a message to pass onto any young man. Start now to pray for God to send you a Christian wife. I did, and I'm glad. God chooses each partner a man or woman is to marry; only God can make a couple, and after that he adds the family. These are rich blessings and should not be taken lightly."

Again, Bradan paused.

"It's only by the grace of God I didn't continue in my folly and die in my sins. God, in his mercy, included me in His way of salvation, and when His son decided I'd strayed enough, held out his hand and lifted me back into the joy of His salvation; and here I am, a picture of God's grace. Every believer in this congregation is a picture of God's grace. God has a pattern for us to live by and it's written for us all to follow in this book," he held up an open Bible. "From now on, I will use this as my guide."

Ken was the first that time with the "Amens."

Bradan returned to his seat where Martha waited with arms wide open. They embraced each other and kissed.

"I'm so sorry, Martha." Bradan hugged her again and Martha made sure their two sons and daughter were included in his embrace.

The Pastor stood and spoke.

"Do you have anything to add, Martha?"

"I have no regrets, Dad."

"I don't believe any of us should have regrets in the outcome of this man's life. He stumbled and has suffered the consequences. There may be consequences in the future, but, thank God, he didn't fall for good and that God didn't cast Bradan off entirely. I firmly believe that what this man went through made a better man, with a greater and stronger testimony.

Bradan, I've never been so privileged to know such a fine man and the woman that loved and stood by you no matter how rough you made the road for her. I believe this proves, further, my theory we need our own school to teach and train our children."

"Thank you, Pastor Asquinn." "Thank you, Dad."

"I think Bradan should be re-established in the fellowship of Golden Ridge Baptist Church. Those that agree raise your hands."

Martin raised his hand, then looked around the sanctuary to see every hand raised. "Unanimous," Tadcu said. "Martha, Charlotte, God truly did mold you two women and prepare you to fill the position of these men's wives. Why else would you be in those positions? Ken, Bradan, both of you are in good standing in this church. Bradan, if you are interested, you can have the position of musical director and song leader back."

"Sure, if Ken's interested in being my assistant." Ken nodded.

Mr. Greene joined Bradan, Martha, the boys and Shannon at the back of the church when the service was over.

"Hello, Chester. It's so good having you come out to church often," Bradan said. "Hello, Bradan Turehue. I've often wondered how those two girls got along after I let them go on account of that accident. I felt I should make the effort to inquire." "If you mean Charlotte and Martha, both are doing fine."

One evening, Ken and Bradan were on patrol, with Bradan driving. The two officers came upon a knot of teenagers grouped together in front of the train station. Some smoked.

"I see Kirby Weston," Bradan said.

Looking guilty, Kirby quickly shoved a tall bottle filled with amber liquid out of sight in a crack in the board platform.

"Uh oh. Looks like a potential trouble spot. Do you think they're drinking?"

"I think they are," Ken replied. "We had better stop and warn them to move on." Bradan slowed, and Ken rolled down his window and spoke to the group. "Move on, don't loiter."

"Aw."

"Police brutality," Kirby complained. "The police always have to come along and spoil our fun."

"Move along, I say," Ken repeated.

The group split up slowly and reluctantly.

When Bradan drove by Chester Greene's property, they encountered some more youths by a small rapid close to the road.

"Looks like the same bunch," Ken said. "Yup," Bradan agreed.

"Slow down," Ken directed.

Bradan rolled down his window. "Didn't we just warn you about loitering and littering?" The group protested mildly.

"It's past curfew and time young people like you were inside."

Ken leaned sideways so he could talk to the group through Bradan's lowered window. "The next time we warn you we will have to talk to your parents."

This time there were no smart remarks or groans of protest. They started towards town and their homes. Bradan turned around and drove back the way they'd just come.

"This is the first time I've driven by here since that awful night Taffy rolled on Gloria.

Even though you said the police said that it was the truck that caused it," Bradan said sadly, "Mr. Greene's still convinced in his own mind that we are responsible for the accident."

"He's appeared to have changed his attitude towards me, and I've tried swaying him otherwise about you not being responsible for the accident. But he simply won't allow his mind to be changed," Ken said.

"Sad," Bradan said, shaking his head. "Ken, do you think Chester's simply trying to free himself of the guilt of being responsible himself for that accident?"

"That's exactly what I think. I think he feels as guilty as anyone, and needs someone to blame. And he's angry that that incident shut down his business. The police told him to sell that horse before." Ken shrugged. "I don't know, if I were him, I'd probably feel guilty and angry, too. I know I've felt guilty all these years believing I'd caused it—and, yet, I didn't really cause it at all. Wish there was some way we could set him free from that guilt. It wasn't him that caused it."

"I noticed Chester working around the stable." Ken nodded. "Turn in there."

Bradan slowed and made the turn into the stable driveway. He parked in the spot he remembered from so many years ago when he and Ken had arrived, drunk, to drive their sweethearts home.

"Chester's not outside," Ken said.

"He musta finished with his chores and went inside," Bradan said.

Bradan pulled up at the back of the house, and parked. He opened the door and stepped out onto the gravel driveway. Ken walked around the hood of the car and strode towards the door with Bradan following. Ken knocked. The two policemen had to wait a few minutes before the door finally opened and Mr. Greene confronted them.

"Come on in," Mr. Greene invited.

Ken and Bradan stepped through to the old man's kitchen. Surprisingly, the linoleum floor was clean, and the kitchen sink free of dirty dishes and the windows let in sunlight from outside.

A cabinet style television stood in one corner of the living-room. "Don't be afraid," Mr. Greene said. "Come on in and be seated."

"A colour TV," Bradan said. "Chester, you must be among the first in this area to own a colour television."

"Colour TV is new to this part of the world," Ken said.

Bradan took a seat on the couch in front of the set. Ken sat in an easy chair. Chester sat back in a recliner.

"I've come to apologize, Mr. Greene," Ken said. Bradan gasped in surprise. "May I call you Chester? We are all grownups now. "

"Certainly. Call me Chester," Mr. Greene consented.

"I've come to say I was drunk that night and in my state I caused enough of a disturbance to make Taffy skittish and do what she did."

Bradan quickly picked up his friend's reasoning. Ken was apologizing to the old man even though they didn't have anything to apologize for in order to keep the peace.

"That goes for me, too," Bradan added. "I wasn't in any kind of a state to be around horses. We take full responsibility for Gloria and her not walking ever again."

Chester Greene was visibly speechless. He looked from Ken to Bradan. "You don't have to say anything," Ken told him kindly.

Mr. Greene said at last, "Well, I never expected you two would finally admit your guilt." "My friend and I came to apologize. Now we'll go."

"We hope you can find it in your heart to forgive us," Bradan said. We're terribly sorry you had to destroy such a beautiful animal."

Chester looked at him, puzzled. "What makes you say Taffy was destroyed?" "Wasn't she?"

"Oh no. No way. Taffy was not destroyed. That was the first idea, but I went to the officer in charge of the investigation that night and begged him to allow me to sell Taffy." I'd received enquiries from a horse-jumping stable that offered me a great price for her. He agreed to let me sell her."

Bradan looked stunned. "And how is Taffy doing?"

"Excellent. I keep track of her career. She's won many championships. She's fantastic and more beautiful than ever. Her professional trainers often comment about how willing she is to have someone saddle and ride her, but she is a strong horse and needs a firm hand."

"Thank you, Chester," Ken said.

"We know that's a compliment coming from you," Bradan said.

"Time to go," Ken said. "Chester, we'll look forward to seeing you in church Sunday."

As Bradan followed Ken back to the cruiser, he felt Chester Greene's gaze on them. He knew Chester watched them until the dust from the car wheels had faded away.

Neither Ken nor Bradan heard the old man mutter, "I will attend services. Yes I will. This Sunday."

TEN
THE ACCIDENT

Grandfather Turehue snapped the gray canvas mailbag onto the hook dangling from an arm of the tower next to the railroad track, then walked down the steps and joined Martha on the ground. Martha and Grandfather Turehue walked back to the cinder platform in front of the railroad station house. The afternoon train from the south announced its arrival with many whistle blasts as it approached Forest Lake.

Martha and Grandfather Turehue waited. The huge brilliant yellow and black diesel engine came into view first. The train slowed to make its way through the town.

"It's slowing, but not enough to stop," the greying man said. Two diesel engines, predominantly yellow in color with black trim, rolled on by, spewing sparks and dust at every turn of the steel wheels. Martha stepped back so the sparks wouldn't land on her skirt or blouse.

The silver-colored mail car immediately behind the engines came into view. The man inside the mail car tossed a heavy canvas bag out onto the cinder platform, almost at Grandfather Turehue's toes. Next, with the ease of experience, the mailman reached out, grabbed the mailbag on the tower and drew it into the car.

This done, he waved at the two on the platform. Martha and her father-in-law waved back as the train faded out of sight behind a rocky ridge with another string of whistle blasts.

Martha and Grandfather Turehue walked across the road to the General Store and Post Office combined. The chimes above the door tinkled as Martha opened the door then held the door open so Grandfather Turehue could go in ahead of her.

She waited while her father-in-law sorted the mail and placed the envelopes in the pigeonholes where they belonged, one for each Forest Lake household. There wasn't much mail today.

"Any mail for us?" Martha asked.

Grandfather Turehue took a fresh fist full of envelopes from the bag, sorted through them and handed some to her.

"Thanks," Martha said

She was about to turn around and go back out the door but Grandfather Turehue's words stopped her.

"I'm taking this fine afternoon off."

"You should. You work far too many hours. I've felt that way since we first moved here." "I had a family to support then. Now there's just Julia and me."

"What will you do with the free time?"

"I'm taking Julia for a canoe ride on Lake Forest." "An excellent idea, Dad."

"Let me just tell, Mrs. Spence."

Martha waited while he gave Mrs. Spence some instructions, then they stepped out into the crisp Autumn air and brilliant sunny afternoon and turned down the road towards home.

"I suppose Bradan is already at work?"

"He's just started the afternoon shift. Dad is counselling a couple, so we don't know when and he will be back. I believe I'll go home with you and stay while you and Mother Turehue prepare for your afternoon."

"And you," Grandfather Turehue asked, "How come you are here and not at your station in Lakeview?"

"My half day off, along with the weekend," Martha answered.

Reaching the Turehues' house, Grandfather Turehue opened the door and stepped aside to allow Martha to enter first.

"Dear, you're home early. Why are you home so early in the afternoon?"

"I have taken the rest of the day off. Mrs. Turehue, you and I are going to enjoy ourselves on the lake this afternoon."

Grandmother Turehue was glad to see her husband in such high spirits. It had been a long time since Martha saw him looking as light-hearted and carefree as he did now and this quickly spread to Grandmother Turehue.

"It's a perfect day for an outing," she agreed.

"It's the kind of September day that calls you to be outside. The golden sun shines down from a cloudless, bright sky."

"Will you get back in time for church this evening?" Martha said.

"We certainly will."

Preparations were quickly completed and soon Grandfather and Grandmother Turehue were at the docks. Martha held the canoe steady while Grandfather Turehue assisted Grandmother Turehue into the front seat and helped her to be seated, then carefully stepped in and sat down in the back seat.

"You are welcome to join us," Grandma Turehue said.

"No thanks. The afternoon is yours and Mom's. Dad, you certainly picked a day to be on the water. The water is such a deep blue and the yellow sunlight just sparkles on the surface." She used the Welsh words for Asquinn Bay. "Wan Asquinn. It all looks so breathtaking from land, but is incomparable when one is right in the midst of it all on the lake."

She looked out across the bay and took a deep breath, savouring the smell of water and forest.

"I like the Welsh words for it, Llwyn Lake."

Then she caught sight of something moving

"I see another boat out on the main body of the lake. There's four young men and a woman. I recognize Kirby Weston. There is a lot of arguing and shouting back and forth. All five must be in various stages of drunkenness."

Uneasiness swept over Martha.

"I wonder where the water patrol officer? Those kids should be in school not on the water."

Martha released the canoe, and with the paddle, Grandfather Turehue touched the side of the dock and pushed out into deep water.

"You two enjoy this fine afternoon," Martha said, "and remember the reef where, Ken, Bradan, me, and Charlotte had been stranded on. It's now marked with a red buoy."

"I'll steer to avoid the rocks," Grandfather Turehue promised.

Martha watched from the dock as the canoe skimmed over the water. This picture was etched in her mind as she watched the two paddle together away from her.

Martha made herself comfortable on the bow of a boat tied up in one of the stalls. Her feet touched the dock.

She saw Grandfather Turehue take off his heavy shirt to be cool.

A family of loons swam to within three feet of the canoe and surveyed them.

Grandmother Turehue's laughter floated over the water to Martha.

Just then, Martha watched with disgust as the speedboat she'd seen earlier passed the canoeists rather recklessly.

The canoeists were out of sight now. Martha turned and started towards home.

Out of sight of Martha, Mr. Greene watched the boatload of rowdies. These eyes beheld that afternoon what no other eyes did.

Later that evening, Martha left her two sons and daughter with Faith, and approached the police station's glass doors. Nimble as a teenager, she climbed the steps into the station. The windows were open to allow in the fresh breeze from the lake. The smell of fresh water and of earth and Fall leaves were strong in the room. Ken and Bradan appeared to be waiting for her by the front desk, and worried. Bradan especially looked as if he felt a premonition of doom.

"Hello. We saw you coming," Bradan said. "Good evening, you two."

"What are you doing here?"

Martha looked at Bradan, and then glanced away. "It's your parents' place." "What's going on there? Is there some kinda trouble?" He asked sharply. His voice quivered as he spoke and the rest of him trembled as if an icy chill gripped his body.

Ken appeared at his friend's side in an instant.

"I noticed it was awfully quiet and still at your parent's place. They went out canoeing this afternoon. I thought they would have been back by now."

"When this afternoon. What time?" Ken asked.

"Four o'clock," I guess," Martha answered. "Grandfather assured me they would be back for church…"

Martha's voice broke and her words trailed off. "And?" Ken prompted.

"They were not in church," Martha said.

"Mr. and Mrs. Turehue likely returned from their unaccustomed fun on the lake, exhausted and laid down for a rest before church," Ken said, "but slept through."

"Please check it out," Martha pleaded. "I just have a really bad feeling about this." "We will do that, Martha."

"Right away?"

"Right away. Let's go, Bradan. I'll drive. You look positively awful." Martha walked outside with the two police officers.

"Look," she said.

When Ken and Bradan looked her way, she indicated with her chin for them to look towards the dock. A dock was in place on the shore in behind the train station. A boat had just docked and five young occupants sat in their seats whooping and hollering. Martha could see the boat and occupants well enough to see it was the same boat she'd noticed before.

"They sure are making enough noise."

"Do you think they have been drinking?" Bradan inquired.

"Certainly sounds like it. We'll find out," Ken declared. He strode towards the railroad tracks, crossed them and started down the sloping trail towards the dock, with Bradan right behind him and Martha trailing a little farther back.

The group saw the two policemen approach. All of them groaned. "What are you all doing?" Ken inquired.

"Nothing," the group chorused.

"You look to me like you have been drinking," Bradan stated. "Oh no," were the answers.

Bradan stepped up onto the dock and stopped in front of the noisemakers' boat and looked inside. Ken came up behind him. Sure enough, empty liquor bottles littered the front.

"Get out of the boat, all of you." Bradan ordered.

The five pulled themselves to their feet, and stumbled their way out of the boat onto the dock.

"Not a one of you can stand up straight," Bradan said. "Come with us. We will hold you in the cell for awhile, at least until you've all sobered up."

"Maybe a long while," Ken said.

The group was escorted to jail and locked up.

Back outside the station, Bradan said, "Get in the cruiser with us, Martha. We'll drive you home."

He helped her into the backseat.

"You are awfully quiet, my friend," Ken said to Bradan as he drove the cruiser through light traffic. "What do you suspect?"

He slowed the cruiser to allow Martha to get out and walk the short distance to the house. "If you don't mind, I'd like to go back to Turehues," Martha said.

She could see the foreboding that had flooded Bradan back at the station had not left him. She could see these feelings balloon as Ken parked in the yard Bradan knew so well and he and Ken got out.

"Beth sy'n gidwydd yma, Bradan mai ffrien?" Ken asked softly as the three looked over the exterior of the house and the yard.

"What's going on here?" Martha repeated Ken's question. "I will tell you what's going on. Grandfather Turehue did tell me when I went to check for our mail this afternoon he's never had much of a holiday."

"That's right, he hasn't," Bradan said.

"He told me he was taking this gorgeous afternoon off to take Mom out on the lake for a canoe ride," Martha said.

"Mom always loved being out on the water," Bradan said. His voice wavered as he finished the sentence.

Ken glanced Bradan's way.

Martha twisted the ends of her dark, waist length hair between the fingers of her left hand. Ken played with the top button of his uniform shirt.

"Your Dad took the afternoon off to take your Mom canoeing?" Ken said.

Bradan nodded. That foreboding feeling was back so strong he could not force words past the burning in his throat.

"Let's go down to the dock," Ken said.

The three climbed back into the cruiser. Ken turned the vehicle around in the yard, and drove out onto the street again. In a few short seconds they stopped by the sandy beach beside the dock.

They left the cruiser parked in a grassy area and walked the few steps to the dock. "Ken, I wonder if that boatload of drunken merrymakers we jailed have anything to do with Mom and Dad not being back?" "I hope not."

Martha's worst fears were realized when they reached the dock. Ken looked sympathetically at his partner.

"The canoe is not in its spot," Martha said. She felt for him as tears started to well up in Bradan's brown eyes.

"Maybe they're just enjoying the day a little longer?"

"A boatload of youth did dock down by the west docks," Bradan said. "We are holding them in cells until they sober up."

"We'll go out in our boat and scour the shoreline and nearby islands for survivors. We have a few hours of daylight yet."

Bradan retrieved paddles from the storage shed, put them carefully inside the police craft, then untied the boat. He and Ken jumped aboard.

"I'm coming, too," Martha said. "I'm a nurse and you may need medical help when they're found."

Bradan tried to take Martha's hand and help her aboard, but Martha brushed it aside and boarded on her own. Bradan waited for her to take a seat before he pushed away from the dock into deeper water. Bradan turned the key in the ignition, and in an instant the boat moved over the waters of the bay towards the main body of the lake.

Once around the fifth point of land, Ken said to him, "Travel close to shore. We will keep an eye open along the shoreline."

A couple of hours later Ken touched Bradan's shoulder and said, "We have scoured to the end of the lake. Think it's time we turned around and went home?"

Bradan nodded.

Martha quickly pointed, "Hey, I see something." Bradan killed the engine.

"In that stagnant patch of muddy, brown water?" Ken asked. "Yes," Martha said.

"All I see is a slimy patch of water with lots of floating weeds and other jetsam," Bradan said.

"We will look," Ken said.

Together the men paddled the craft to the spot. The two put their oars in the water and paddled backwards in order to stop the boat.

"I'm right," Martha said. "Here, we will use this net to retrieve it."

She picked up the net from where it lay on the bottom of the floor by the back seat and dipped it in the slimy water. She came up, the first time, with what she wanted. Martha gasped and her head spun when she recognized the object. She glanced at her husband.

"The hull of a canoe," he said. "Look, the name Turehue. That's part of the bow of my father's canoe. The canoe must have been smashed to smithereens on that reef out there."

"But how?" Ken asked.

"There haven't been any high winds all day," Martha said. Ken touched his partner's shoulder in sympathy.

"There is no reason why any canoe or boat should meet a fate like that today," Bradan said as if he hadn't heard his partner. Martha noticed he had a difficult time controlling his emotions and temper.

"Unless, unless…." Bradan's sentence trailed off.

"Unless what?" Ken said."I know what you are thinking."

"Unless another boat with its occupants so intoxicated they couldn't see what was going on around them was involved," Bradan filled in. "Why weren't those delinquents removed from the lake?" Bradan continued. "Making sure the lake is safe for everyone is not our job."

"Bradan, calm down," Ken said, gently. "We aren't sure yet anything has happened to your parents."

"Then where are they? Why is Dad's canoe smashed to smithereens? Both Mom and Dad are experienced boaters; they would not pile up on a dangerous reef in calm weather like this on their own. Someone else has to be involved."

"I don't know, Bradan. Maybe they are simply somewhere on an island waiting to be rescued."

"What simpler explanation could there be?" Martha said. "It's too simple an explanation," Bradan snapped. "Constable, we must search for survivors," Ken said.

An hour later Bradan slowed the boat to avoid rocks.

"This is the last island before entering Wan Asquinn and home," Martha said. "And we've found nothing of your parents," Ken said.

A while later Bradan brought the boat gently alongside the dock. The three occupants climbed out of the boat onto the dock and secured it.

"It's the end of our shift now, we, or I, will pick this up tomorrow," Ken said. "You are to take a few days off. I'm taking you off this case, Constable, my friend. You are too closely involved."

"But..."

"No buts. I'm ordering you off these proceedings. You are to go home and I don't want to see you around the station, or crime scene, until your parents are located. There is no option.

Understood?"

"Yes, sir."

When they arrived at Ken's place, Martha found Charlotte, Faith and her companion, Bradley Olverton, Mamcu and Tadcu, and the children under one roof.

Ken kissed Charlotte.

"Ken, I'm so glad you're home," Charlotte said.

"You girls have perfected the art of getting together when Bradan and I are at work," he joked.

Bradan hugged Charlotte. Oh, what was he to tell her? He agonized within.

"We certainly have. Especially when our husbands work the afternoon, or grave yard, shift," his sister agreed. She turned to Faith, "Thanks for baby-sitting."

"You're welcome," Faith answered. "I love babysitting my nephews." Bradan looked around for a distraction.

"Hi, Daddy," he heard Gerald call from the living-room.

Bradan continued into the front room with Mamcu, Martha, Ken and Charlotte trailing.

The three boys were dressed for bed.

"Hi, Daddy," Gerald greeted his father. "Hi, Daddy," Lyle greeted him cheerfully. "Da. Da," Brian said.

"How are you?" Bradan asked Gerald. "Fine, Daddy," Gerald said.

"We missed you, Daddy," Lyle said.

"And I missed you all," Bradan assured the youngsters. He hugged them all. He checked his watch. "It's past your bedtime."

"Bedtime, children," Martha said and the children noisily made their way to their bedrooms.

Charlotte turned to her brother. "Whatever is wrong? You certainly are not brimming over with your usual joy of life."

"His usual zeal for life has been drained from him," Faith agreed. She looked at Bradley sitting beside her on the couch. "Something's wrong, I can feel it."

"There certainly is," Bradley said.

Martha didn't answer. She didn't feel it was her place to tell what the Ken had wanted kept under wraps for the time being.

Bradan groaned inwardly. What was he to tell Charlotte?

Eleven
God's Green Pastures

Martin found them when he entered the house. Olvina clung to one of Audrey's hands while Phoebe clung to the other. Eunice took his hand while Cassia held onto her hand, and Kathleen grasped her father's other hand.

Faith sprang to her feet. "I will look after those sweet girls for you for a while," she offered. Bradley joined her.

"I want to help," he said.

One at a time, Faith picked up a toddler and Bradley set each one down on the couch. Martha signalled Martin to follow her in the kitchen.

"Did you hear the news?" Martha asked the instant they were seated at the kitchen table. "About Mr. and Mrs. Turehue?" Martin said.

"Yes," Martha said.

"That's why we came over," Martin said. "We thought Charlotte wouldn't want to be alone. But, I see she isn't alone. She has crowds for company."

"The more the merrier," Martha said.

"Ken has taken my husband off the case," Martha explained further. "He thinks Bradan is too close to the case."

"He is," Martin agreed. "And Ken did the right thing." Martin leaned back in his chair, closed his eyes and prayed.

I pray that what I fear, and I know Ken does, will turn out not to be true. Let Winston and Julia Turehue be safe on some island, waiting rescue.

But the chill that ran down his spine told him this was not so.

Father, I bow to thy will. Whatever has happened is best in thy sight. If Winston and Julia have died tonight, then they are happy in heaven with you."

After the prayer, Martin felt much more at ease and peace. A conviction overtook him, ever so quiet yet distinct.

Be of good cheer, my child. It is true Bradan's parents have died. Do not fret for I will be with him and his sister through this difficult time. Their parents are with me in heaven.

Martha heard loud voices in the front room and allowed her twin to lead the way back to the living room. He saw Ken glance at him questioningly and Bradan answer with a shake of his head. Martha did not miss any of this; neither did Martin or Charlotte.

"What's wrong?" Charlotte asked.

Ken and Bradan glanced at each other again. Ken cleared his throat, but no words come out.

Concern showed in Charlotte's hazel eyes. "What is it?" Bradan looked at Ken. "Shall I tell her?"

Ken nodded. "You first."

Bradan cleared his throat. "Martha came to the office this afternoon." This raised Martin's eyebrows. "Oh? What for?"

Feeling miserable, Martha glanced at her twin. This was the hardest night of her life, trying to keep quiet and act as if she didn't know anything had happened. She couldn't keep quiet any longer.

"I thought it was awfully quiet around Mr. and Mrs. Turehues' place, and felt Ken and Bradan should investigate. Earlier today, Mr. Turehue told me he was taking the rest of the day off, since it was such a beautiful Fall afternoon, so he could take Mrs. Turehue on the lake for a canoe ride."

"Mom and Dad had promised to be back in time for evening service, but didn't return.

And that's when Martha came to us," Bradan said Bradan's voice failed him and Martha continued.

"I asked Faith to babysit the children and went to the house, and there was no one home." "I will tell the story from here," Ken said. "We went down to the dock below Golden

Ridge and discovered your Dad's canoe was not in its place. That's when I thought we should start looking for Mr. And Mrs. Turehue, as well as other clues. We discovered a portion of your dad's canoe with the name Turehue painted on it."

Ken paused, looked at Bradan, indicating he should take over the telling of the story. "That's when Ken and I went out on the lake to try and locate Mom and Dad." "Try?" Charlotte croaked through the tightness in her throat.

It was the hardest sentence Ken ever had to form.

"We did not find your Mom and Dad. All we found was a part of the canoe. It must have gotten smashed up on that reef by Fifth Point."

"You didn't find them?" Charlotte gasped.

"Are you saying Mr. and Mrs. Turehue drowned?" Martin asked.

Bradan had to turn away. He stood with his back to the others in the room, fighting for control. Ken was forced to answer.

"That's exactly what we are afraid of," Ken stepped in again, "although it hasn't been confirmed yet."

"Oh, yes it has," Martin whispered. Ken and the ladies glanced at him.

"What do you mean?" Charlotte wanted to know.

"I have been praying all this afternoon and have heard the Lord's voice confirm that they are with Him."

"Me, too," Martha said.

Charlotte put a hand over her mouth. "Oh, no." Martha went to her friend and hugged her.

Bradan took his wife his arms. Charlotte clung to her husband, sobbing and sniffing.

All of them clung to one another, offering what condolences they could. For a long time no words were necessary.

Bradan spoke first. "Time to wake the children and go home."

Ken interceded. "Why don't you all sleep here tonight? I think we need to be together as a family right now."

Martha nodded.

"Good idea," Bradan agreed.

"I will need to be well rested to interview Kirby and friends first thing in the morning," Ken said. "I'm going to have busy, full days for a while since we'll need to continue searching for the Turehues. Our next step, since their bodies haven't been found on shore, so far, is to drag the bottom of the lake."

The next day Martin was seated in the kitchen, along with Bradan, Mamcu and Tadcu. He looked out the living-room window and saw Chester Greene, of all people, approaching the house.

As word had spread about the tragedy, there'd been a steady stream of church members and neighbours bringing gifts of food, flowers and condolences. But Martin never expected to see Mr. Greene among that group.

Chester Greene entered. He set a pan of cinnamon rolls on the kitchen table, already laden food.

"Glad you came," Charlotte greeted him.

"It's a blessing to have the church behind us at a time like this," Bradan said, gratefully.

The next morning Ken arrived at work. His first concern was the prisoners.

"You are all looking good to me. I will have breakfast delivered for you, then I'm going to interview you, one by one."

Breakfast over, Ken interviewed the female prisoner first. He went to her cell where she stood by the door alone. He inserted the key, opened the door, and after handcuffing her, walked beside her to where he would interrogate her.

The room held one table, two chairs and a light bulb hanging from the ceiling above the table.

"Sit down. What's your name?" Ken invited. "Fiona," answered the lady.

"Well, Fiona, if that's your real name. I need you to tell me what you and your friends were out on the lake yesterday afternoon, the afternoon of October 15."

"It's hunting season," Fiona answered. "The boys wanted to check out the possibility of shooting a moose this year."

"But it was a school day," Ken said. "So?" Fiona shrugged.

"The four of you had been drinking," Ken continued. Fiona didn't answer.

"Did you see anyone else, another boat on the lake?" Fiona didn't answer.

"You didn't see a small craft with an elderly couple as passengers?" No answer.

Ken sighed. He tried again. "This elderly couple are husband and wife, enjoying a gorgeous afternoon canoeing on the lake, but they've disappeared. We are searching, but have had no luck so far locating them. Can you help us?"

Fiona turned away. She laid her arms on the table and buried her face in them. She did not attempt to answer.

Ken stood up, pulling Fiona with him. "Where are you taking me?"

"Back to your cell. I have three others to interview."

After the interviews, Ken didn't know any more about Bradan's parent's whereabouts than before.

The telephone rang and Bradan answered it on the first ring. Martha went to the telephone with him and stood with her arms around his waist.

"Turehue residence, Bradan speaking."

"How are you, my friend? How are you and Martha holding up?"

"Fine, thanks, Ken. How has your day been so far?"

"Did you find anything out from the four suspects?' Bradan asked.

"No," Ken said. "I interviewed the four, separately, but their united answers were all the same. No one saw another craft on the lake yesterday afternoon. Their stories are too pat. It's as if the girl, she's a bit older than the male suspects, coached the rest what to say. We're holding them as this investigation continues. Because of lack of evidence, I'm calling this a 'drowning accident'. I've heard from the officers involved dragging the lake. There are no reports of anything of value being brought to the surface. I'm going out there as soon as I'm through talking with you."

"Then I had better not keep you."

"Bye, Bradan." The two friends hung up. Bradan sat back in his easy chair.

"Did the police find anything?" Martha said.

Bradan shook his head. "I'm afraid not. Ken's holding the four boaters from yesterday afternoon. He's forced to call it a boating accident."

This brought a gasp of disbelief from Charlotte. "Why?"

"Because of lack of evidence to be able to charge them for murdering or being otherwise involved in the disappearance of our parents."

That brought a snort of disgust from Martin. "I don't believe it!" Martha laid a comforting hand on his shoulder.

Bradan jumped to his feet.

"I feel so helpless. I wish Ken had allowed me to remain on duty and help." "He was wise to take you off the case," Martha pointed out.

"You are too closely, emotionally involved," Martin added.

Bradan was into the second day of his forced time off. He lounged on the couch, feet resting on a footstool when the telephone rang. Bradan sat up straight, reached out and snatched up the receiver.

"Hello?"

"Hello, Bradan, my friend." "What's up, Ken?" Bradan said.

"Are you tired of days off?" Ken asked.

"I can't stand sitting around here anymore waiting. I was just about to go outside for some fresh air and a walk," Bradan said.

"I have plenty for you to do," Ken said. "Just tell me," Bradan said.

"I need more officers to keep any kid or adult from crowding too close to the edge of the rocks and falling into the lake. I need you down here ASAP. Meet me at the dock below Golden Ridge in three minutes."

"Yes, sir."

Bradan hugged Lyle, Gerald, and Shannon good-bye, then Charlotte. He quickly buckled on his equipment belt holding his pistol, nightstick and handcuffs around his waist.

Bradan held out his arms to embrace his wife, but Martha said, "I will walk to the dock with you."

Bradan nodded.

He and Martha arrived at the dock the same time as a police boat. Martha walked up to Ken and asked, "Is it all right if I join you?"

"Absolutely," Ken said. "Just make sure you stay way back from the cliff's edge and don't interfere with the investigation."

Bradan and Martha climbed aboard the police boat. The driver used the paddle to push away from the dock. The boat whisked away across the bay, around the point and soon slowed down at a spot where the rocks were level with the water.

Martha followed Bradan onto the outcrop of rock. Martha watched as the boat backed away and turned to skim back to where the men searched the lake.

"Over here," Bradan said. "There's a trail fishermen use to get close to the water to fish." On top of the steep cliff, Bradan crossed the yellow "Do not cross. Police crime scene" tape and strode towards onlookers lining the cliffs, watching the police drag the lake below. "Police. I need you to step back," he said to the first bunch of curious onlookers, then continued edging his way through the crowd.

Martha found a safe spot where she could peek over the cliff's edge. The height made her head swim. So did the rocks showing above the water. She turned away. Bradan faced the onlookers.

"Police. Away from the edge of the cliff, please," he urged.

Much to Bradan's relief, the crowd moved back away from the cliff's edge without argument.

"What's happened, sir?" one man asked.

"We aren't sure yet," Bradan answered. "It's best you all go home and hear what happened on the news. We don't want any of you to end up on the rocks below."

When the crowd had cleared the area, Bradan and Martha went back down the steep trail they'd climbed up, and joined the officers in the boat. The two of them were whisked away across the bay to the dock in front of the railroad station.

"Please, don't leave us yet, Martha," Ken asked. "Will you be available if we need you for something concerning the case?"

"I will be keeping Bradan company at the police station," Martha answered.

At nine-fifteen in the evening, after the late northern Ontario sunset, the radiophone sputtered.

"Are you there? Bradan? Martha?" Bradan and Martha exchanged nervous glances.

Bradan hesitantly reached for the receiver. "We're here."

"I'm calling the search off for the night," Ken said. "I will meet you at the dock below Golden Ridge."

"Yes, Ken," Bradan answered. He shut off the radiophone, shut down the computers and covered them carefully with plastic coverings, then he and Martha went outside. Bradan locked the door and the two started the walk towards the dock.

They joined Martin and a crowd from the church gathered at the dock below Golden

Ridge.

Bradan and Charlotte automatically sought comfort from each other. Bradan had one arm around Charlotte's waist, and she rested her head on his shoulder.

They waited like this as the patrol boat's bright light appeared. The boat docked and Ken got out.

"Goodnight, sir," Constable Bates said. "Goodnight, Constable Turehue." He tipped his hat to Martha. "Goodnight, Ma'am."

"Goodnight, Constable," Ken answered. "We will widen the search area." "Did you find Mom and Dad?" Charlotte asked.

"Not yet, sorry." Ken said, sadly.

Mamcu and Martin walked the short length of dock.

"I'm off duty now. I'm going home and have a good rest until daylight."

Mam and son embraced. Mam released Ken and he moved on to Charlotte. Bradan released Charlotte, and she ran to his outstretched arms. He embraced her and hugged her to him tightly.

"Anything?" Bradan said.

Ken shook his head wearily and squeezed his friend's shoulder. Martha took her husband in her arms and hugged him.

"I'm calling this a drowning accident," Ken said.

"Murder would be more like it," Charlotte voiced her opinion.

"I understand how you might feel that way," Ken said, "but there's no evidence showing that they were murdered. Let's all head home."

And so it went for the rest of the day, and the next. But one day was different.

The sun shone straight down on Bradan and Martha. White, puffy clouds drifted in a deep, blue sky. It was lunch hour and they were on their way home for lunch. Bradan and Martha met Martin returning from the schoolhouse for his lunch hour. He fell into step beside Martha as they came to the front door of Ken's house as this was where they all gathered.

"How was school?" Martha asked.

"It was okay," Martin answered. "The students enjoyed pulling weeds in the school garden and generally preparing the soil for next spring's planting."

When the three entered the kitchen of Ken's house, Mamcu set a plate full of food in front of each person.

"Because there's so many, the children were fed earlier," she said lightly, in an attempt to lighten the mood.

Martin pushed his away. "I'm not hungry."

Mamcu set full plates of food in front of Martha, Bradan and Charlotte. Bradan started eating immediately.

"Thank you," he said.

"Thank you," Martha said. She, too, started eating hungrily. Charlotte looked at the food and made a face, then pushed hers away.

"But you have to eat," Mamcu said, frustrated. "You have to keep your strength up."

Charlotte pulled the plate in front of her again and reluctantly began to eat. She'd cleared the last bite from the plate when the telephone in the front room shrilled. Everyone seated at the dinner table jumped and then glanced nervously at the instrument and then at each other.

Bradan looked first at Martha then Charlotte. "Uh oh," he said.

The telephone continued to ring.

"I'll answer that, if you want," Martin offered. Bradan shook his head. "It might be Ken."

Bradan pushed away from the table, made his way into the living-room and picked up the receiver.

"Constable First Class Bradan Turehue speaking. Oh, hi, Ken."

There was a brief but deep silence from Ken. Bradan listened, breathless, with everyone else in foreboding anticipation.

"We found them. We raised your parents' bodies from Lake Forest a few minutes ago."

"Where?"

Bradan asked.

Charlotte put a hand over her mouth and Tadcu tightened his grip on Mamcu.

"A long distance from where the accident occurred. Both drifted into a bay on the west shore."

Bradan remained calm.

"You need me and Charlotte down there to identify the bodies, don't you?" "Yes. Meet me at the police station. How soon can you and Charlotte get here?" "We will be there in five minutes."

Bradan hung up. Charlotte rushed to his side. Bradan held her tight but not a tear of anguish escaped from the eyes of either one.

"Hang in there," Bradan said. "We have no reason to be sad. We know now Dad and Mom are enjoying the glories of heaven."

"I know. I know."

The congregation of Golden Ridge Baptist Church had gathered again for one of their mid-week services.

From his seat with his family, Martin looked up at the podium where Bradan stood, leading the song service. Martin could see that Bradan was not happy with the singing. They all seemed crushed and very sad—defeated.

Bradan held up his hands.

"Stop singing. Everyone, stop, please."

The whole congregation stared at him, wondering what was going on.

"I know the church has lost two cherished members. Please don't be overwhelmed with shock and grief over my parents' death. We all should rejoice because Jesus has taken another of His children home to be with Him.

"Amens," echoed throughout the sanctuary.

"We will start this hymn over again and sing it with praise and glory to Our Maker." He looked at the organist.

"All right, Esther."

After that, the singing was shouted out with praise and joy, instead of being held down with heaviness and sadness.

The little church overflowed with praise and happiness that evening.

From where he sat, Martin saw some passersby pause and listen to the sounds coming from the church.

It was the day of Grandfather and Grandmother Turehues' funeral. Together Ken and Bradan sang Heaven *MUST BE A BEAUTIFUL PLACE*, then Bradan sang a solo, *I'LL BE THERE*. As the second hymn concluded, Ken and Bradan lifted the guitar straps over their heads, set the instruments against the wall and left the platform. Martin took their place.

"I will be speaking the eulogy," he began. "To begin with, I felt nothing but joy and great pleasure and comfort to be in the presence of both Grandfather and Grandmother Turehue.

"Winston and Julia Turehues' lives were cut off earlier than they should have been. But they didn't die, they merely fell asleep and their children can rest in the knowledge they now are alive with the saints in heaven. Charlotte and Bradan can rejoice, knowing that they will see their parents in heaven. There is no real sorrow here, friends and relatives that knew the Lord as their own personal Saviour will see the two in Glory."

Charlotte and Bradan got up from their seats at the same time and joined him. Charlotte hugged her brother-in-law, tears running down her cheeks. Martin stood aside as Bradan talked.

"My parents will not have to endure endless toil and persecution on this earth anymore," Bradan continued. "Whether it's a happy or sad day depends on one's standing with God. If a child of God, and if walking in harmony with His precepts, then it is a happy day; if one has not experienced the saving power of God through salvation, then it is a sad day. I rejoice and I can say it's a happy day for our parents because our parents walked with God."

The three returned to their seats, all wiping tears from their eyes with Kleenexes. The pastor stepped behind the pulpit. "If there are no more tributes, we will proceed outside to the graveyard."

When no one spoke up, Ken positioned himself at one corner at the end of Grandmother Turehue's casket while Bradan grasped the opposite corner. Eric and Tim claimed the middle.

Vincent was alone at the front, but not for long as Chester Greene positioned himself next to the younger man.

When the pall-bearers were ready, the caskets were lifted up and the procession started down the aisle and to Tadcu and Mamcu waited, and set on the ground before him.

"Precious is the death of one of God's saints," the pastor began. "Today we have two of them. It is with sad and heavy hearts we say goodbye to Mr. And Mrs. Turehue today. The two that had been partners in life are now partners in death. Together they enjoy the glories of heaven."

As the backhoe started lifting dirt back into the grave began, the crowd began to break up. Some gathered in groups for a talk before going to their cars and driving off. Bradan and Charlotte remained by the graveside, Charlotte's face buried in the material of Bradan's tuxedo. Martha waited with Ken in the parking lot.

At last Charlotte moved away from her brother, together they started towards their spouses.

The day after the funeral, a full moon shone down from a partially cloudy sky upon Bradan and Martha as they stepped out of their house.

"It's nice of Charlotte to look after, Ger, Lyle and Shannon while we go for a walk together," Martha said. "Thanks for inviting me to walk with you."

"I felt you need to get out of the house," Bradan said. It's the day after dad and mom's funeral, the school is closed for three days. All of us are on bereavement leave, but you, it seems. You've been spending all your time making sure everyone else is okay."

Bradan and Martha crossed the tracks and made their way down the bank to the docks.

Without thinking about it, side by side they walked to where Bradan's father's brand new canoe, hand built by Martin, Ken, and Ricky had once been moored. Martha spied the name piece of her father-in-law's canoe lying on the dock. She walked over to it, picked it up, turned it over in her hands several times, looking at the name. Then with a cry of anguish, she raised her arms to fling the piece of wood high into the air, but before she could toss it, Bradan grabbed her arms.

"This is a piece of evidence. Don't throw it away."

Martha hesitated, then dropped the piece of wood. It landed with a clatter on the dock. Together they looked out over the water of the bay.

"What did happen the evening my parents died?" Bradan said in a whisper.

Martha touched her husband's shoulder and whispered, "Look, someone's sitting on a fallen tree trunk on one of the points of land, close to the water, watching us."

The figure waved.

"It's Chester Greene," Bradan said. Martha let out her breath, relieved. "I think he wants to talk to us."

"Let's use a canoe and paddle over there," Bradan said.

They climbed into a canoe moored alongside the dock and paddled quickly up to the rocks where the old man sat and brought the canoe alongside. Chester Greene jumped to his feet to hold and steady the canoe while Bradan climbed out, then secured the front rope around a small, nearby tree.

"Good evening to you, Chester Greene," Bradan said and shook hands with the other man.

"What are you doing out here on this treacherous stretch of cliffs and all by yourself?" Martha asked.

"Just enjoying the peace and quiet," Chester Greene answered.

"Hmm," Bradan said, "you must see a lot going on the lake from here?" "You could say that," Chester Greene said.

"You didn't happen to be on this stretch of the shoreline the night my parents died?" Bradan asked.

Chester Greene's faded blue eyes clouded over, and he hesitated in his answer, "Why?

There were no witnesses, therefore not enough evidence to hold them. " Martha glanced at Bradan, confused.

"Hold who?" Bradan asked. He jumped on his opportunity. "Chester, what are you trying to tell me?"

Chester Greene rambled on. "They all claim they did not see anyone else on the lake." "Maybe they didn't see anyone else," Martha began.

"Shh," Bradan cautioned her, "Don't interrupt." Bradan turned to Chester Green, "Chester, tell me what you saw."

"They were likely too drunk and two people in a small canoe are not easy objects to spot.

But I know the fools were goofing off, speeding and making circles."

"How do you know that?" Bradan asked.

"I stood on this very point the day of the boating accident," Chester Greene said. "I could see everything, even open liquor containers in the boat. They saw the canoe with two people in it.

"I heard Kirby Weston shout, 'It's Mr. And Mrs. Turehue. They are members of the church Pastor Asquinn pastors, therefore enemies of ours. They are friends of the very people meant to die in a fire we brought on through witchcraft. Instead, my father's house burned down, and my oldest brother died.'

"Each sentence became louder and louder as bitterness took over." Bradan looked at Martha. Both shivered.

The hatred Kirby bore towards Christians in Golden Ridge Baptist church must have been deep, Bradan thought.
"They started shouting and hollering, rocking the boat, making circles and waves as close to the canoe as possible. It wasn't long before the waves carried the canoe up against the rocks and smashed the frail craft. Your parents sank, never to resurface."

Bradan drew a deep breath. "I came out to try and find out what went on, for my own satisfaction, not for vengeance against those likely responsible. Deuteronomy 32:35 tells us we are not to seek vengeance. In the New Testament in Romans 12:19 the words say, 'Dearly beloved, avenge not yourselves, but rather give place onto wrath: For it is written, vengeance is mine: I will repay, sayeth the Lord'. I do realize the evidence. The reef is clearly marked by a red buoy. Let Jesus take care of the situation."

"That's a good attitude to have," Chester Greene said. Martha shivered. "I'm cold."

"But what you just told me is very plain evidence of murder," Bradan said, ignoring Martha. "Chester, you did the right thing coming to me about what you saw. You could have been arrested for withholding evidence. If I neglect reporting what you've told me, my future could be in jeopardy. Be at the police station tomorrow morning and I'll take a statement from you."

"I sure will be," Chester agreed.

Bradan turned to Martha, "We should get home."

Bradan and Martha climbed back into the canoe, and Bradan paddled off into the moonlight.

He looked back at the spot where they had just talked to Mr. Greene, but, even in the bright moonlight, Bradan did not see him.

The next morning Ken and Bradan barely had time to settle at their desks when Chester Greene made his appearance.

"Ken," Bradan said when his partner glanced curiously his way when Bradan reached for a pad and a pencil. These he handed to Chester Greene. "He's here to write and sign a statement. Last night he sought me out to get something off his chest."

Ken read through the old man's writings when Chester Greene finished. "Are you willing to tell all this in court?' Bradan asked.

"I sure am," Chester Greene said. "Then sign it," Bradan said.

Chester Greene signed the statement and pushed it across the desk to Bradan. "You are free to go," Bradan said.

Alone in the police station, Ken looked at his partner. Bradan braced for a reprimand. Ken had ordered him not to get involved with the investigating part of the case.

"Steller job, my friend," Ken said.

Bradan breathed easier. "We won't need a warrant for the arrest of the four suspects. This is not private property."

In the cell area, four sad human beings hung their heads in remorse as they heard Bradan's words. "You four will be charged with negligence, having open alcohol containers in your boat, and failure to cooperate with an investigation associated with Mr. and Mrs. Turehue, and for their murder."

Not too many days after the suspects were charged, Bradan Martha, Charlotte, and Ken gathered in the one-roomed school house. Others had gathered but only to listen. At the front, a lawyer sat at the teacher's desk, a briefcase resting against the chair legs at his feet.

"And to my two children, Bradan Matthew and Charlotte Julia, I leave the house and everything in it."

Bradan and Charlotte clapped their hands in their joy. Ken and Martha joined in. The meeting broke up shortly, and the school house quickly emptied.

The short walk to homes began. Those living further from the school climbed into vehicles and drove away.

Eric, his wife June and Gay-Anne caught up with Bradan just before Eric turned into where he lived.

"I'm glad I caught you before you passed our place," Eric said. "Is there something urgent on your mind?" Martha said.

"Sort of," Eric replied.

"Out with it, then," Bradan urged.

"What are you going to do with the store and house?" Eric said. "The store, I will sell," Bradan said without hesitation.

"Not interested in being a store master?" Martha asked. "No. I'm a policeman," Bradan said. "I love my job." "And the house?" Eric said.

"Why?"

"The quints are growing fast, and Sihon is still with them, Martin's eager to start renovating the upstairs apartment for the girls use. I've asked God to open up a way and find a house for us. So far, nothing."

"Then your hunt is over," Bradan said. "I won't refuse you if you want to buy the house."

"I do," Eric said.

"Then you and your family join us for dinner tomorrow evening and we will work out the details."

"We will. Thanks, Bradan."

"That will be wonderful," Charlotte said.

In church the following Sunday morning, Chester Greene could not sit still in his seat. He shook and trembled. Martin made his way quickly to his pew.

"Chester, would you feel better if you talked to me?" "I think I would."

Martha rushed to where Mr. Greene sat and stood beside her twin. "I feel God is telling me I need to repent of my sins."

Martha put a hand over her mouth. "I'm so thrilled."

"Are you clear on the plan of salvation? I mean God's plan of salvation," Martin asked softly.

"I know there is no other way to be saved but through Jesus Christ. The Father sent him to die on the cross for my sins; we are bought and redeemed through His shed blood on the cross."

"I believe you do," Martin said.

"Astonishing, isn't it?" Mr. Greene said. "God used Ken's and Bradan's lives to help show me how awful my life has been due to my grumpiness and stubborn ways."

"And, through my father's unwavering preaching, you have come to know the true way of salvation," Martha said.

"Jesus died to save me, one of the elect, by the drawing of the Holy Spirit," Mr. Greene said.

With Chester between Martin and Martha, the twins rejoiced along with the rest of the church members, and the angels in heaven sang in triumph, as The Great Shepherd sought and found another of His own, and brought him into the fold.

www.ingramcontent.com/pod-product-compliance
Lightning Source LLC
Chambersburg PA
CBHW070054120526
44588CB00033B/1433